A Few of My

FAVORITE THINGS

A Few of My FAVORITE THINGS

Recipes Inspired by Family-Friendly Musicals

VEEDA BYBEE

SHADOW MOUNTAIN PUBLISHING

Dedicated to my favorite of favorites:

the Awesome Bybees

Interior Art Credits: p. 4, 8, 36, 64, 94, 124 Nadezhda Deineka/Getty Images; 5, 9, 37, 65, 95, 125 Aleutie/Getty Images; 11, 55, 144 Vadim /Adobe Stock; 12 Rogatnev/Adobe Stock; 15 incomible/Adobe Stock; 16, 87 Pure Imagination/Adobe Stock; 19 Agussetiawan99/Adobe Stock; 20, 43, 105 MaksimYremenko/Getty Images; 23, 121 ngvozdeva/Adobe Stock; 24, 109, 143 WinWin/Adobe Stock; 27, 72, 84 Alfmaler/Adobe Stock; 28, 63 Heather Ward; 31, 51 AnnaPa/Adobe Stock; 32 brgfx/Adobe Stock; 35, 97, 118 Lili Kudrili/Adobe Stock; 39 zarica/Adobe Stock; 40, 75 Marina Zlochin/Adobe Stock; 44, 147 Vector Tradition/Adobe Stock; 47, 56, 101, 102 Sergii Pavlovskyi/Adobe Stock; 48, 140 vivali /Adobe Stock; 52 Arcady/Adobe Stock; 59, 67, 76, 110, 151 EVGENIY/Adobe Stock; 60, 98 Stockgiu/Adobe Stock; 68 Stockgiu/Adobe Stock; 71, 155 SpicyTruffel/ Adobe Stock; 79, 92 poppystyle/Adobe Stock; 80, 156, 159, 160 Миша Герба/Adobe Stock; 83, 88, 114 mything/Adobe Stock; 91, 122 pingebat/Adobe Stock; 106, 139 viktorijareut/Adobe Stock; 113 foxysgraphic/Adobe Stock; 117 Ilona/Adobe Stock; 127 artoptimum/Adobe Stock; 128 vectorikart/Adobe Stock; 131, 136 Svetlana/Adobe Stock; 132, 148 studioworkstock/Adobe Stock; 135 defarmerdesign/Adobe Stock; 152 Little J/Adobe Stock.

Visit us at shadowmountain.com

Library of Congress Cataloging-in-Publication Data

Names: Bybee, Veeda, author.
Title: A few of my favorite things : recipes inspired by family-friendly musicals / Veeda Bybee.
Description: [Salt Lake City] : Shadow Mountain Publishing, [2024] | Includes indexes. | Summary: "Author Veeda Bybee presents recipes inspired by family-friendly musicals."—Provided by publisher.
Identifiers: LCCN 2024023865 (print) | LCCN 2024023866 (ebook) | ISBN 9781639932993 (trade paperback) | ISBN 9781649333032 (ebook)
Subjects: LCSH: Cooking. | Musical films. | BISAC: COOKING / Courses & Dishes / General | COOKING / Methods / Quick & Easy | LCGFT: Cookbooks. | Literary cookbooks
Classification: LCC TX714 .B94 2024 (print) | LCC TX714 (ebook) | DDC 641.5—dc23/eng/20240705
LC record available at https://lccn.loc.gov/2024023865
LC ebook record available at https://lccn.loc.gov/2024023866

Printed in China
Regent Publishing Services Limited, Hong Kong, China
10 9 8 7 6 5 4 3 2 1

CONTENTS

Introduction 1

OVERTURE
Essential Ingredients and Favorite Kitchen Tools 5

OPENING NUMBER
Breakfast 9

ACT I
Supporting Characters:
Sides, Salads, and Dressings 37

INTERMISSION
Snacks and Beverages 65

ACT II
Entrees 95

FINALE
Desserts and Toppings 125

Index 163

Musical Index 169

Introduction

For a good portion of my life—mainly the formative time of my children's growing-up years—I did not like musicals. This is a cookbook devoted to recipes inspired by musical theater, so you can already guess the narrative arc.

I wasn't always so grumpy toward the jazz hands production numbers and catchy melodic show tunes. In high school, I was a theater kid. I played the alto saxophone in the orchestra pit for many shows, helped with art direction, and painted and designed numerous sets. My senior year, I decided to be brave and get myself to the front of the stage. Despite the fact that I'm no great singer, I joined the chorus for our school's performance of *Grease*.

My best friend in high school had season tickets to Shenandoah University's musical theater performances in Winchester, Virginia, and I was lucky enough to be her family's plus one. I was introduced to *Guys and Dolls*, *Gigi*, *My Fair Lady*, and so many more. Between these college-level performances and the occasional trip to the Kennedy Center in Washington, DC, where I saw Broadway productions of *Beauty and the Beast* and *The Phantom of the Opera*, I had so much exposure to good musical theater. I loved the music, the dancing, the sets—all of it.

Over time, I didn't feel like the theater loved me back. As an Asian American, I didn't see people who looked like me on stage. The film productions that did feature an Asian cast were either whitewashed or had storylines with uncomfortable stereotypes. Almost unknowingly, I turned my back on Broadway. I buried the joy of hearing the chorus line or the excitement of the last song of Act I.

Once I became a mother, this disdain for music in storytelling carried on. We were *not* a house that watched musicals. The Bybees did not listen to the soundtracks in the car. We weren't people to watch musical movies on Sundays, or spontaneously burst into song in a unified choir. We became a family that did not like musical theater. Or so I thought.

Without my encouragement, my children quietly gravitated towards these singing and dancing productions. They asked to try out for community shows. They had friends and extended family in musicals, and they were also attracted to the spotlight. In elementary school, my two older children got their feet wet acting in *Mary Poppins* and *School of Rock*. Like most kids in 2016, they started listening to the *Hamilton* soundtrack—over and over and over again. By this point, my cold, small heart began to grow.

When the COVID-19 pandemic put a pause on regular life in 2020 and every day was Blursday, we decided to make the live stage recording of *Hamilton* a family event. While this score of hip-hop, jazz, R&B, and Broadway tunes had been stuck in our heads for years, this would be the first time anyone in our household would see the play.

Beginning with "Alexander Hamilton," the opening song in Act I, we were quickly transported to the year 1776, with a cast reflective of these current times. The energy of the play was infectious, and I was swept up in the story and music. Seeing Phillipa Soo as Eliza Hamilton, Leslie Odom Jr. as Aaron Burr, and Lin-Manuel Miranda as Alexander Hamilton was powerful. This onscreen visibility of BIPOC actors was meaningful. My heart grew one more size. I felt the spark of something old shine through. Watching *Hamilton* was a breath of fresh air I didn't know I needed.

With kids in online school and no social plans whatsoever, I came up with a recurring family activity: We would watch a musical every Friday for a year and cook dishes inspired by those shows. It was the kind of ambitious goal you could only do when the world turned upside down. During these days of social distancing, our Family Musical Fridays became a bright spot to our repetitive weeks of isolation. I came up with criteria for these family musical nights:

1. The musicals had to be family-friendly productions that were accessible to view from home. This limited us to productions already on film.
2. There needed to be a diverse representation. I found that the best way to be inclusive was to search for recent remakes. For instance, for *Grease*,

we watched the TV stage production of *Grease Live!* (2016) with Vanessa Hudgens as Rizzo and Jordan Fisher as Doody.

3. In my recipe research, I wanted to cook food either mentioned in the musical or something close from that time period.

4. I made my own test for musicals: If there were at least two songs and one dance number, it was a musical!

As I searched for shows that were inclusive in cast and story, cooking from these productions was transformative. Again, my heart grew once more, and I went from feeling indifferent and grinchy about musical theater to planning our lives around them. I selected musicals most of my family hadn't seen before. For ones we were *all* unfamiliar with, I'd research the food.

Note: There are a few Asian-inspired musicals. While I love my Asian American heritage and the excellent food from my culture, I do not find much inspiration in the representation in these musicals, especially the older films. I've included a smattering of Asian recipes and hold on to hopes that one day there will be reason for more.

This collection highlights some of our favorite shows, including others that were already family favorites. The recipes included are also some of my most treasured. From the show-stealing Pickpocket Cardamom Bread Pudding (see page 19), tweaked from a recipe passed down from my mother-in-law, to the Lazy Morning Congee (rice porridge) I ate growing up (see page 27), these are truly some of my favorite recipes. I hope they will find a place at your table—and maybe during a night of watching musicals, too.

OVERTURE

A French word for *opening*, the overture is the introduction to the musical, usually a medley of the various tunes that will be part of the production—or the prep work that will take place before the show . . . or in the kitchen. This section covers the basics needed for cooking.

Essential Ingredients and Favorite Kitchen Tools

In-Stock Pantry 6

My Favorite Kitchen Tools 7

Miscellaneous Essentials 7

Essential Ingredients and Favorite Kitchen Tools

IN-STOCK PANTRY

All-purpose flour: We usually purchase our AP (all-purpose) flour in large, restaurant-sized bags from the bulk stores. I almost always sift my flour before use to be ultra-careful about clumps.

Canola oil: My neutral oil of choice; it's versatile for cooking, frying, or baking.

Chocolate chips: We keep a big, restaurant-sized plastic bucket of semisweet chocolate chips in the pantry. We use this chocolate for cookies, melting for bark—and snacking straight from the container.

Dijon mustard: The handiest mustard around. Yes, it's great for sandwiches but even better to thicken and emulsify salad dressings.

Dutch-processed cocoa powder: Unsweetened with a deep chocolate color and flavor, cocoa powder is an essential base for most from-scratch chocolate recipes.

Extra-virgin olive oil: High in monounsaturated fats, this earthy and fruity tasting olive oil is a healthy choice for cooking. High quality oil is used best when drizzled over dishes, and whisked into a salad dressing.

Kosher salt: These large, flakier grains of salt are my main seasoning for cooking and baking. Instead of making food salty like table salt, kosher salt helps to enhance flavors. My tastebuds love salt, so I tend to season more liberally. In the majority of the recipes I will say "season to taste." There is a difference in brands, so taste test along the way.

Large eggs: When a recipe calls for eggs, these are the size I use. For baking, using room temperature eggs will help ingredients like flour and butter cream together more smoothly.

Neutral oils: Vegetable oils like canola, safflower, sunflower, or peanut don't leave a strong taste like olive oil or avocado oil can.

Nonstick cooking spray: Sprayable oil to coat cake pans or baking sheets so food won't stick.

Soy sauce: Salty, bitter, sweet, this is an essential condiment to add umami, or savoriness, to a dish.

Sugar: To satisfy my sweet tooth and to be ready for stress baking, it's almost guaranteed there will be plenty of granulated (white) sugar, light brown sugar, and confectioners' (powdered) sugar in the pantry.

Unsalted butter: Using unsalted butter helps control the sodium levels of a recipe, since salted butters can have varied salt content. However, I *do* use salted butter—especially when making frosting.

MY FAVORITE KITCHEN TOOLS

Baking Tools

- Baby whisks
- Fine-mesh strainer
- Offset frosting spatula
- Pastry brush
- Rolling pin
- Rubber spatula
- Spatula
- Whisk

Baking Pans

- cooling racks
- 8 x 8 metal baking pans
- 8½ x 4½ metal loaf pans
- 9-inch pie plates (glass)
- 8-inch round metal cake pans
- 9-inch round metal cake pans
- 9 x 13 baking pans
  (both ceramic and glass)
- 18 x 13 half-sheet baking pans
  (sometimes called jelly roll pans)

MISCELLANEOUS ESSENTIALS

Essential consumables: parchment paper, aluminum foil, plastic wrap, toothpicks, bamboo skewers, ziptop plastic bags (quart- and gallon-size), paper baking cups

Knives: chef's knife, paring knife, bread knife, and cutting boards

Pots and pans: large soup pots, Dutch ovens, large skillets, cast iron pans, medium-sized saucepans, small-sized saucepans

Prep tools: prep bowls, measuring spoons, liquid measuring cups, dry measuring cups, rasp grater (such as Microplane), vegetable peeler, citrus juicer, box grater, can openers, food scale, heatproof flexible spatulas, baby spatulas, whisks, baby whisks, oven mitts, dish towels

Small appliances: blender, microwave, food processor, stand mixer, handheld mixer, immersion blender

OPENING NUMBER

Setting the stage for the performance, the first song of a play welcomes the audience to the theater. Like a good start to a show, these dishes can also set the tone for the rest of the day (and can be eaten for supper as well).

In our household, breakfast isn't distributed like fast food, where pancakes and hashbrowns are served until the cutoff time of 10 a.m. We don't limit these dishes to the morning rush. I'll sometimes make Baroque French Toast Sticks for an after-school treat, or Good Morning Puffy Oven Pancakes as a weekday meal. Breakfast, eaten at any time, wins hands down.

Breakfast

Baroque French Toast Sticks
Beauty and the Beast 11

Good Morning Puffy Oven Pancakes
Singin' in the Rain 12

Henry Higgins's Proper Full English
My Fair Lady 15

I Am the Pumpkin King Bread
The Nightmare Before Christmas 16

Pickpocket Cardamom Bread Pudding
Oliver! 19

Let's Twist Cinnamon Sugar Donut Bites
Hairspray 20

Spoonful of Sugar Strawberry Drop Scones
Mary Poppins 23

Maui's Coconut Syrup
Moana 24

Lazy Morning Congee
Turning Red 27

One Last Time Honey Hoe Cakes
Hamilton 28

No Worries Banana Bread
The Lion King 31

Frog Prince in the Hole
The Princess and the Frog . . 32

Baked Banana Blueberry Oatmeal
Song of the Sea 35

SERVES 4

8 slices Texas toast

4 eggs

1 cup heavy cream

2 teaspoons vanilla extract

3 tablespoons granulated sugar

2 teaspoons ground cinnamon

½ teaspoon kosher salt

Neutral oil for frying
(like canola or vegetable)

Toppings

One batch Big Top Whipped
Cream (see recipe on page 160)

Sliced fruit

Confectioners' sugar

Maple syrup, optional

Toasted almonds, optional

Baroque French Toast Sticks

Baroque, which arrived in the English language from a word in French meaning "irregularly shaped," is a fitting title for this breakfast recipe. In France, pain perdu is basically days-old bread drenched in a custard mix. These Baroque French Toast Sticks become a twist on pain perdu when topped with whipped cream, sliced strawberries, and toasted almonds. Dusted with confectioners' sugar, this recipe can also work for an American viewing of Singin' in the Rain.

We use thick slices of Texas toast to make generous-sized portions, perfect for dipping in saucers filled with warm maple syrup. They are a little bit French, a lot American, and the simpleness of this recipe needs no fixing.

Cut each slice of toast into three thick pieces lengthwise. Each section will be large, like a thick french fry.

In a shallow rimmed dish such as a pie pan, whisk the eggs. Once mixed together, add the heavy cream and vanilla extract. Continue to whisk and stir in the sugar, cinnamon, and salt.

Coat a nonstick skillet or cast iron pan with oil and heat over medium heat. Dip the bread slices into the custardy egg mixture and flip to coat completely. Add custardy bread in batches to the skillet and cook until golden in color, about 1 minute on each side. Serve warm with whipped cream, sliced fruit or berries, and dust with confectioners' sugar.

SERVES 6

½ cup (1 stick) salted butter

6 eggs

1½ cups milk

1½ cups all-purpose flour

½ teaspoon kosher salt

3 tablespoons granulated sugar

⅛ teaspoon (or a pinch)
ground nutmeg

1 teaspoon vanilla extract

Good Morning Puffy Oven Pancakes

I have my mother-in-law, Norma, to thank for passing along this family recipe. Or should I give proper attribution to my sister-in-law Erin, who gave me a binder of Norma's recipes for Christmas one year? Either way, we have oven pancakes because of the Bybee women, and it has made our kitchen table a better place.

Essentially a large, puffy pancake divided up into portions, it's great for feeding a family. With a quick zip in the blender, this batter comes together fast. While cooking in the hot oven, it will puff up tall, like a fluffy pancake cloud. They deflate quickly and are best eaten right away.

This dish has several names such as German pancakes or Dutch babies. With their Western European roots, they work for a Sound of Music *showing or a good breakfast choice for* Singin' in the Rain. *Good morning to you!*

Preheat oven to 450 degrees F. Put the stick of butter into a 9x13 baking pan. Place the butter and pan in the oven. While the butter melts, make the batter. The timing is important on this, so watch to make sure the butter doesn't begin to burn.

In a blender, mix the eggs until blended. Add milk, flour, salt, sugar, and nutmeg, and continue mixing until incorporated, about 30 seconds. Add the vanilla.

Remove pan from oven and pour batter into the melted butter. Place back in oven and bake for 20–25 minutes until puffy and golden. The pancake will deflate soon after it's removed from the oven. Serve immediately topped with fruit, powdered sugar, lemon juice, or syrup.

MY FAIR LADY
also *Mary Poppins Returns*

SERVES 6

1 batch (2½–3 cups) cooked You'll Be Back British Baked Beans (see recipe on page 63)

1 (12-ounce) package sausage links

1 (12-ounce) package bacon

Oil for frying

1 dozen eggs

3 heirloom tomatoes, sliced in half

Kosher salt and fresh ground black pepper

6 slices white or wheat bread

Butter, room temperature

Henry Higgins's Proper Full English

When our family was young, we spent two months living in London during a college externship. I fell hard for the city and its culinary surprises. I adore the foreign-to-me-eating beans in the morning with toast. Overall, I consider this a close rendition of a full English. It doesn't really matter how you plate this fry-up as long as beans are in the middle.

It's become a Father's Day tradition for breakfast, and something we call the Full English Brendan. While the kids still don't like seared tomato halves, we can all get around strips of swiggly bacon. I take some liberties by toasting the bread instead of pan frying, omitting sautéed mushrooms, and using regular bacon instead of back bacon. If curmudgeonly Professor Higgins from My Fair Lady *was ever stateside, I think he would approve.*

There are two ways to prepare this breakfast. The first is to cook the main elements (beans and sausage and bacon) the night before, and warm them up as you're frying the eggs and tomatoes. The second way—cooking everything the day of—I'll explain here. While it's possible to put it together yourself, it can be fun to include other family members to help plate or cook one element of the breakfast.

Make the batch of You'll Be Back British Baked Beans (see recipe on page 63) and keep warm on low heat until plating.

Heat two cast iron pans or nonstick skillets over medium heat, or use a large electric skillet on medium heat. In batches, fry the sausages in one pan and the bacon in the other until the sausages are brown and the bacon is crispy. Remove from the pans and pat with paper towels, covering with foil. Drain the grease from the bacon pan and add a small amount of oil to the sausage pan, just enough to coat the pan.

Fry six eggs in each pan, working in batches of two and season to taste. If you'd like your eggs over easy, cook for a minute on each side; for sunny side up, cover with a tight lid and cook on one side for about 1½ to 2 minutes. Add salt and pepper to taste. As the eggs are done, place one serving (¼ to ½ cup) baked beans on the center of a plate, then add two eggs to the bottom of each.

When the eggs in the first pan are done, begin the tomatoes. Place the tomato halves cut side down and fry about 30 seconds to sear. Add to the plate. Plate two strips of bacon and two sausage links near the top of the plate. Toast the bread and butter generously, cut in half and place on the upper portion of the plate or on a separate plate. Serve everything immediately. Cheers!

OPENING NUMBER: Breakfast

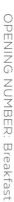

THE NIGHTMARE
BEFORE CHRISTMAS
also *Alice in Wonderland*

MAKES TWO
9x5-INCH LOAVES
or five 5x3-inch
mini loaves

Unsalted butter for preparing pans

3⅓ cups all-purpose flour
+ extra for flouring pans

3 cups granulated sugar

2 teaspoons baking powder

1 teaspoon ground cinnamon

1 teaspoon freshly grated nutmeg

1 teaspoon ground cloves

1½ teaspoons kosher salt

4 eggs

1 (15-ounce) can
(or 2 cups) pumpkin puree

1 cup canola oil

⅔ cup water

1½ cups semisweet
chocolate chips

I Am the Pumpkin King Bread

Another recipe to give my mother-in-law, Norma, recognition for: her pumpkin bread. As this pumpkin bread bakes, it fills the kitchen with the sweet scent of cinnamon and nutmeg, and it feels like you are wrapped up in autumn. Cakey and soft, it's hard to eat just one slice—or wait till the leaves turn orange to bake this. I find myself breaking out this pumpkin bread recipe in the month of September, even before it officially becomes fall. Okay, fine—August.

A great breakfast, dessert, or anytime snack, this is a great pumpkin recipe to give homage to Jack, the Pumpkin King, from The Nightmare Before Christmas. *This bread also is a wonderful teatime treat for watching* Alice in Wonderland.

Preheat oven to 325 degrees F. Butter and flour two 9x5 loaf pans or five 5x3 mini loaf pans and set aside.

In a large bowl, whisk together the flour, granulated sugar, baking powder, cinnamon, nutmeg, cloves, and salt. Set aside. In another bowl, beat the eggs. Add the pumpkin puree, canola oil, and water and mix until incorporated. Fold in the dry ingredient mixture, mixing only long enough to combine. Stir in chocolate chips.

Pour the batter into the pans and bake for 35–40 minutes for mini loaves, 70–90 minutes for large loaves, or until the sides of the loaf pull away from the pan. For the large loaves, once the timer hits 70 minutes, you can check on the bread every couple of minutes. Insert a toothpick into the loaf to check for doneness—a few crumbs will cling to the toothpick. I like mine more on the moist side.

SERVES 12

Butter or nonstick baking spray

1 (16-ounce) loaf challah bread

1½ cups granulated sugar

1 tablespoon orange zest
(from one medium-size orange)

6 eggs

2 teaspoons ground cinnamon

½ teaspoon ground nutmeg

1 teaspoon ground cardamom,
freshly ground preferred

1 teaspoon kosher salt

3 tablespoons orange juice

4 cups milk

1 cup heavy cream

2 teaspoons vanilla extract

Toppings

1 batch Barnum's Salted Caramel
Sauce (see recipe on page 159)

1 batch Big Top Whipped Cream
(see recipe on page 160)

1 (2.25-ounce) package
chopped pecans

Pickpocket Cardamom Bread Pudding

I need to be careful with cardamom. I love this complex, citrusy spice so much I want to add it to everything. Like a pickpocketing orphan, cardamom can steal the show, adding warmth and depth to recipes, especially baked goods. For this cookbook, I've practiced restraint, using cardamom sparingly. Paired with the zest of sweet oranges, this versatile spice brings out the other flavors of cinnamon and sugar.

While most leftover loaves of bread will do, challah, the specialty braided loaf of Jewish origins, is a great option for this dish. Rich from egg yolks and butter, the texture of challah bread is fantastic for bread pudding, and a viewing of Oliver! *For extra oomph, use freshly ground cardamom, ground right from the seeds. You can use a spice grinder or food processor to blitz the spice into fine particles. Spiked with the freshy ground cardamom and topped with rich caramel sauce, it will have the people around you saying, food, glorious food!*

Preheat oven to 325 degrees F. and place rack in center of the oven. Grease a 9x13 pan with butter or cooking spray.

Cut challah bread into 1-inch cubes. Place bread pieces into the buttered pan.

In a bowl, add sugar and orange zest. With your fingers, rub the zest into the sugar until fragrant. In a separate large bowl, whisk the eggs until frothy. Stir in zested sugar, cinnamon, nutmeg, cardamom, and salt. Next, mix in the orange juice, milk, cream, and vanilla. Pour the wet mixture over bread cubes. Bake for 65–75 minutes or until top is golden brown. Serve warm with desired toppings.

MAKES ABOUT
30 DONUT BITES

Donuts

Nonstick baking spray

¾ cup granulated sugar

Zest of one lemon

2 cups all-purpose flour

1 teaspoon baking powder

¼ teaspoon baking soda

½ teaspoon kosher salt

½ teaspoon ground nutmeg

1 teaspoon ground cinnamon

½ cup (1 stick) unsalted butter, melted

¼ cup canola oil

½ cup sour cream

1 egg

1 teaspoon vanilla extract

Cinnamon Sugar Mix

½ cup granulated sugar

1 teaspoon ground cinnamon

3 tablespoons melted unsalted butter

Powdered Sugar Mix

½ cup confectioners' sugar

3 tablespoons melted unsalted butter

Let's Twist Cinnamon Sugar Donut Bites

If you need to know one thing about the Bybees, it is that you can win our hearts with donuts. The over-the-top ones piled with frosting and sprinkles are fun, but we also hold appreciation for the traditional classics. Donuts are, in fact, Grey's favorite food.

This recipe is a variation of a cake donut; instead of fried, these are baked in a mini muffin pan. The "donuts" don't come out perfectly circular, but holy moly, like a song in Hairspray, *this is a dish you can take right to the bank. They are wonderful rolled in cinnamon and sugar or powdered with confectioners' sugar. These donut bites can be a sweet way to start the morning or possibly a pick-me-up in the afternoon.*

Preheat oven to 425 degrees F. and lightly spray a mini muffin pan with nonstick baking spray.

In a large bowl, add the sugar and lemon zest. With your fingers, rub the zest into the sugar. The oils from the zest will make the sugar soft and smell wonderfully citrusy. In the bowl of lemon-scented sugar, whisk in the flour, baking powder, baking soda, salt, nutmeg, and cinnamon. Stir in the melted butter, oil, sour cream, egg, and vanilla.

Fill the muffin pan cups about halfway with the batter. If you want a circular top, roll the dough into 1½–2 inch balls and place in muffin cups. Bake for 8–10 minutes, or until a toothpick inserted into the center comes out with just a few crumbs. Cool in pan for a few minutes, then remove to rest on a wire rack.

Meanwhile, make the cinnamon sugar mix in a shallow dish such as a pie pan by tossing sugar together with the cinnamon. Brush the donut holes with butter, then roll in the cinnamon sugar mix or confectioners' sugar and serve.

MARY POPPINS
also *Alice in Wonderland*
or *Song of the Sea*

MAKES 8–10

2 cups all-purpose flour

½ cup granulated sugar

4 teaspoons baking powder

½ cup (1 stick) cold salted butter cut into ½-inch cubes

1 egg

½ cup heavy cream, plus more for brushing

Water

1 cup strawberries, diced

Glaze

½ cup confectioners' sugar

2 tablespoons heavy cream

Coarse sugar, such as sanding, pearl, or demerara, for dusting (optional)

Spoonful of Sugar Strawberry Drop Scones

British/Irish scones are flaky and oh so ethereal and tender. One bite and, like George Banks in Mary Poppins, *you'll feel like you're floating away on the string of a kite. Shaped with spoonfuls of dough, the scones bake up in a craggily circle shape. Slathered with jam, butter, or clotted cream, this soft, crumbly quick bread is laced with pockets of chopped strawberries and can be dusted with sugar. They're wonderful for breakfast, an afternoon tea, or any time you want to take your taste buds to the highest of heights.*

Preheat oven to 425 degrees F. and place the rack in the center of the oven. Line two half-sheet baking pans with parchment paper and set aside.

In a large bowl, whisk together the flour, sugar, and baking powder. Add the cold butter, mixing into the dry ingredients with a pastry cutter or your fingers. After mixing, the flour/butter mixture should be coarse like sand or small pebbles.

In a separate bowl, whisk the egg and heavy cream together. Fold the wet ingredients into the flour/butter mixture. The batter will be thick and wet. If it seems too dry, add water a tablespoon at a time.

Next, gently fold in the diced strawberries until just combined. If overworked, the strawberry juice will bleed and color the scones pink.

Place scoops of dough, about ⅓ cup each, onto the parchment-lined half-sheet baking pans. Brush the top of each scoop with heavy cream.

Bake for 12–15 minutes until golden brown. As the scones bake, make the glaze. In a small bowl, whisk together ½ cup of confectioners' sugar and 2 tablespoons of heavy cream. Remove scones from the oven and allow to cool on a wire rack.

Drizzle or brush the warm scones with the glaze. Sprinkle the optional coarse sugar over the glazed scones. Serve warm or at room temperature.

MOANA
also *Singin' in the Rain*

MAKES 2 CUPS

1 (13.5-ounce) can coconut milk

1 cup granulated sugar

Maui's Coconut Syrup

Faced with the greatness of this simple but rich and delicious syrup, breakfast may never be the same. Made with just two ingredients, it's adorable how easy this recipe is. Creamy and full of coconut flavor. It can transport any breakfast to the islands—or at least help set the stage for a viewing of Moana. *You're welcome.*

Pour coconut milk and granulated sugar into a medium saucepan. Place pan over medium heat and whisk until the sugar is completely mixed into the coconut milk.

Once the mixture starts to boil, turn the heat down to medium-low. Let the syrup simmer for about 15–20 minutes, stirring occasionally to prevent burning. The syrup will reduce and thicken slightly. As it cools, it will thicken more. Serve warm or cold.

TURNING RED
also *Mulan, Scrooge,* or *Oliver!*

SERVES 8

1 cup uncooked rice, long grain preferable

1 quart water

2 (32-ounce) cartons (2 quarts) chicken stock

1 teaspoon kosher salt

Flavorings
(optional if making plain gruel)

1 tablespoon minced ginger

2 tablespoons fish sauce or soy sauce

White pepper, to taste

Toppings (optional)

Fried garlic

Fried shallots

Cooked shrimp

Cooked shredded chicken

Cooked ground pork

Sliced green onions

Sliced egg omelet

Lazy Morning Congee

Growing up, rice soup (or congee) was my Asian American family's sick day meal of choice. It was our version of chicken noodle soup! Simmered in a combination of chicken stock and water, the rice soup becomes a base for bright flavors like sharp ginger and savory meat.

As the rice breaks down, it becomes thick and creamy. Adding in an umami burst of fish sauce, white pepper, and sliced ginger transforms a basic porridge into a meal to serve for a movie night of Turning Red *or* Mulan. *Throw in proteins like cooked chicken, sliced omelet, or sautéed vegetables, and this blank canvas becomes a filling meal, flowing with flavor.*

If you wanted to stay true to the bland theme of gruel in Oliver! *or* Scrooge, *serve congee (or rice porridge) plain with absolutely no toppings or condiments. I suggest not sticking too closely to the time period and updating this to a wonderful Asian breakfast congee.*

In a large soup pot or Dutch oven, boil the rice, water, chicken stock, and salt over medium heat.

Once the soup comes to a boil, lower the heat to medium-low. Keep covered for 30–45 minutes, or until the porridge is bubbly and about to boil over. Stir often to prevent the rice from sticking to the bottom of the pot.

Turn the heat down to low and partially cover the pot with half the pot lid. Continue to cook for another 20 minutes, or until the soup is thick and creamy. The rice will look soft as the grains expand. Stir in 1 tablespoon of grated ginger and 2 tablespoons fish sauce or soy sauce. Add white pepper and more fish sauce or soy sauce to taste.

Remove from the heat, add desired toppings, and serve hot.

HAMILTON
also *The Princess and the Frog*
or *Singin' in the Rain*

SERVES 6

1 cup all-purpose flour

1 cup finely ground
yellow cornmeal

1 tablespoon baking powder

½ teaspoon kosher salt

1 tablespoon brown sugar

2 eggs

2 tablespoons honey

1 cup buttermilk

¼ cup canola oil, plus
more for frying

Toppings

Honey

Maple syrup

1 batch Maui's Coconut Syrup
(see recipe on page 24);
add in ½ teaspoon of
rum-flavored extract

1 batch Big Top Whipped
Cream (see page 160)

One Last Time Honey Hoe Cakes

For our Family Musical Friday viewing of Hamilton, *I did a deep dive into the 1700s and discovered that hoe cakes, also called griddle or corn cakes, were George Washington's favorite food. Knowing this, I knew this dish absolutely needed to go into our musical night.*

Hoe cakes are delicious served with jam or berries, and also taste great with warm honey, syrup, or apple butter. Topped with sliced bananas, pecans, whipped cream, and coconut-rum-flavored syrup will turn these hoe cakes into a New Orleans–style Bananas Foster treat to accompany a viewing of The Princess and the Frog.

In a large bowl, whisk together flour, cornmeal, baking powder, salt, and brown sugar. In a separate bowl, beat eggs with honey, buttermilk, and oil. Add these wet ingredients to the large bowl of dry ingredients, stirring until batter is combined.

Heat a heavy skillet or cast-iron pan over medium heat. Add about 1 tablespoon oil, just enough to coat the bottom of the pan.

Drop about ¼ cup of batter into the hot pan, and repeat to fit about 3 to 4 hoe cakes in the pan. Cook on each side until golden brown. Repeat for the remaining hoe cake batter, adding more oil to the pan as needed. Allow the cakes to cool on a wire rack and serve warm with toppings.

MAKES 1 LOAF
(ABOUT EIGHT SLICES)

Nonstick baking spray

½ cup (1 stick) unsalted butter

3 ripe bananas

2 eggs

½ cup plain Greek yogurt

1 teaspoon vanilla extract

2 cups all-purpose flour

¾ cup granulated sugar

1 teaspoon baking soda

1 teaspoon ground cardamom

1 teaspoon ground cinnamon

½ teaspoon kosher salt

1 cup semisweet
chocolate chips (optional)

½ cup chopped walnuts (optional)

No Worries Banana Bread

During our time of staying at home all day every day, one of the recipes the kids liked to make by themselves was banana bread. In our house, we always seem to have bananas on the edge of no return. While brown bananas aren't ideal to slice or eat raw, when they're overripe, they're perfect for banana bread.

Flecked with cardamom and cinnamon, this sweet bread has a lingering, citrusy, spicy flavor that blends well alongside the possible addition of chocolate chips. (Grey would remind you chocolate is not optional.) With the addition of yogurt, this quick bread bakes up soft and dense. Great for the king of the Pride Lands, but it also slices up prettily for an Alice in Wonderland-*style tea party.*

Preheat oven to 350 degrees F. Coat a metal 9x5 loaf pan with cooking spray and flour.

In a small glass or ceramic bowl, heat butter in microwave until melted, about 30 seconds to one minute. Set aside and let cool.

Remove bananas from peels. In a medium bowl, smash bananas until pureed. We use a potato masher, but a fork, the edge of a cup, or even your hands will work. Once the bananas are gooey, whisk in the eggs, yogurt, vanilla, and melted butter.

In a large bowl, whisk together flour, sugar, baking soda, cardamom, cinnamon, and salt. Using a rubber spatula, fold the smashed banana mixture into the dry ingredients. Gently mix until combined with no flour streaks. If using chocolate chips or walnuts, stir in.

Pour batter into the floured loaf pan. Bake for 50–60 minutes, or until a toothpick inserted into the middle comes out with just a few crumbs attached.

Once done, allow to cool in the loaf pan on a wire rack for about 10 minutes. Run a plastic butter knife between the loaf and the pan and then let rest 30 minutes to an hour. Remove from pan. Slice and serve.

SERVES 4

4 slices bread, such as white
or wheat sandwich bread

Salted butter or canola
oil for frying

4 eggs

Kosher salt and pepper

Frog Prince in the Hole

While the English version of Toad in the Hole is made with sausage links peeking out of a layer of Yorkshire pudding, this American rendition spins an identity of its own. Also called Egg in a Hole, Egg in a Basket, or Egg in a Hat, this dish is essentially a fried egg cooked in a cut-out hole of sliced bread. I like using regular sandwich bread for this recipe; I prefer the thickness of precut slices. The bread is also soft and makes cutting out the center easier as well.

Note: there are no real toads or frogs used in this recipe. This is a good dish for watching The Princess and the Frog, *where none of the main characters are actual amphibians either.*

With a round cookie cutter—or even the rim of a drinking glass—cut a circle out from each slice of bread, then toast the bread circles. Butter the circles and set aside.

In a large skillet over medium heat, melt butter or add in oil, just enough to coat the pan. Place the slices of bread with holes in the pan.

Crack an egg into the hole of each slice of bread, careful not to break the yolk. Season with salt and pepper. Cook until the bread starts to brown in the pan, about one minute. The bottom on the egg and the toast should be a golden-brown color. Flip the toast and egg over gently, cooking on both sides.

Serve immediately alongside the toasted and buttered bread circles.

SERVES 8–10

½ cup (1 stick) unsalted butter, plus more for greasing the baking dish

2 cups steel-cut oats

1 teaspoon ground cinnamon

¼ teaspoon ground nutmeg

1 teaspoon baking powder

½ teaspoon kosher salt

½ cup brown sugar, plus 2 tablespoons for sprinkling

5 cups boiling water

½ cup heavy cream

1 teaspoon vanilla extract

1 cup blueberries

1 banana, peeled and sliced

Baked Banana Blueberry Oatmeal

My husband, Brendan, is part Irish/Scottish/English and French. With my Asian heritage, our mixed-race kids are happy to have ancestorial ties to both Lunar New Year and St. Patrick's Day.

This baked version of oatmeal is something I like to wake up to. Anything made in an oven has my heart, and I appreciate the scents that ping-pong across the house when something's cooking. I really like the addition of sliced bananas and whole blueberries. Steeped in oats, the banana releases a wonderful flavor, and the blueberries give each bite a fruity burst. This is great on a cold weather day or snuggly morning—a perfect meal to imagining you are by the chilly seaside, watching Song of the Sea *or even* Darby O'Gill and the Little People.

Preheat oven to 375 degrees F. and place rack in the center of the oven. Butter a 9x13 baking dish.

In a large pot, melt the butter. Toss in the steel-cut oats and stir until toasted, about 3–5 minutes. Add in the cinnamon, nutmeg, baking powder, and salt, and continue to stir for one more minute. The oats will be toasty and fragrant. Mix in the ½-cup of brown sugar. Pour the boiling water on top. Stir in the cream and vanilla.

Place oats in the 9x13 baking dish and drop in the blueberries and bananas. The bananas will float to the top of the oatmeal mixture. Sprinkle the top of the oatmeal with the remaining 2 tablespoons of brown sugar, making sure to top the banana slices with brown sugar.

Bake for 50–60 minutes or until the oatmeal looks slightly firm and cooked. The oats will still be a little soft. Let cool for 15 minutes and serve warm with cream, or more sugar.

ACT I

At award shows, there's a reason recognition is given to supporting actors. They may not be the main attraction, but with their assistance, a show shines with depth and nuance. Just like the supporting character in a Broadway play, these side dishes can enhance any meal, helping the main course sing.

Supporting Characters: Sides, Salads, and Dressings

Bob Cratchit's Smooth Mashed Potatoes
Scrooge 39

Guardian Ginger Orange Dressing
Mulan 40

Corny's Crab Cakes with Tartar Sauce
Hairspray 43

Santa Cecilia Street Corn Cups
Coco 44

Anatevka Potato Latkes
Fiddler on the Roof 47

Garden Envy Cauliflower Soup
with Hazelnuts
Tangled 48

Hakuna Yamatata Berbere Fries
The Lion King 51

King Brian's Butter Boiled Potatoes
Darby O'Gill and the Little People 52

Castle Feast Lemon Vinaigrette
Beauty and the Beast 55

Hawaiian Mac Salad
Lilo & Stitch 56

Going the Distance Feta Cheese Fries
Hercules 59

Triton's Salade Niçoise
The Little Mermaid 60

You'll Be Back
British Baked Beans
Hamilton 63

SERVES 8–10

5 pounds Yukon Gold potatoes

1¼ cups cream, heated and warmed

1 cup (2 sticks) unsalted butter, room temperature

2 teaspoons kosher salt, plus more to taste

Freshly ground black pepper

¼ teaspoon garlic powder (optional)

Bob Cratchit's Smooth Mashed Potatoes

Typically, I'm not in favor of kitchen tools that have only one function. However, a potato ricer, used for making mashed potatoes, deserves a place in kitchen cupboards. It has a dedicated space in mine.

If you aren't familiar with a potato ricer, don't be alarmed at its bulky appearance. Resembling a medieval weapon, this potato ricer crushes the potatoes extra fine, creating air as it pushes cooked potatoes through small holes. It helps contribute to the smooth and creamy texture that makes these potatoes so irresistible. If you don't have a potato ricer, you can also use a potato masher.

For this side dish, I prefer Yukon Gold potatoes. They have a great yellow color and creamy potato filling. Heating the cream before adding it also ends up with silkier results. If you want to bump up the flavor, add a little optional garlic powder.

These potatoes are great on their own for Scrooge *or the American classic* Annie, *where Little Orphan Annie eats this side dish during her first night at Daddy Warbucks's mansion. Or use this as the top layer of Emerald Isle Shepherd's Pie (see recipe on page 97) to celebrate a viewing of* Song of the Sea.

Peel and cut potatoes into quarter pieces, about 2-inch chunks. Add potatoes to a large pot of salted, cold water, filling a few inches above potatoes. Over medium heat, cook the potatoes until soft enough to pierce with a fork, 30–35 minutes.

Meanwhile, heat cream in a small saucepan or microwave. Set warm cream aside.

Drain the cooked potatoes into a colander. Place the potato ricer over the large pot and pass cooked potatoes through in batches. After all the potatoes are riced, add butter into the pan. Stir to melt. Next, add the warm cream a little at a time. Add the two teaspoons of salt, mixing the potatoes while still hot helps keep them creamy and smooth. Add additional salt and pepper and optional garlic powder to taste. Transfer to a large bowl and serve warm.

MAKES ABOUT 1 CUP

¼ cup orange juice

1 tablespoon rice wine vinegar

2 teaspoons honey

2 tablespoons granulated sugar

1 teaspoon grated ginger

1 tablespoon Dijon mustard

2 teaspoons orange zest

½ cup extra-virgin olive oil

½ teaspoon kosher salt

Freshly ground black pepper

Guardian Ginger Orange Dressing

This Asian inspired dressing is sweet, citrusy, and bright, a good accompaniment for a crunchy slaw of cabbage and carrots or any greens. The addition of ingredients like rice wine vinegar and ginger give this flavoring its Asian fusion flare. Used over salad, it can be served as a side during a viewing of Mulan *or* Turning Red.

Whisk the orange juice, rice wine vinegar, honey, sugar, ginger, Dijon mustard, and orange zest together. Slowly drizzle in the olive oil and continue to whisk until emulsified. Season with salt and pepper to taste.

MAKES 8 CRAB PATTIES

1 pound jumbo lump crab meat

½ cup mayonnaise

1 large egg, beaten

2 tablespoons freshly squeezed lemon juice

1½ teaspoon Old Bay seasoning

1 teaspoon Dijon mustard

1 tablespoon Worcestershire sauce

¼ teaspoon kosher salt

½ cup panko breadcrumbs

Canola oil for frying

Lemon wedges for serving

Tartar Sauce
Makes about 2 cups

1 cup mayonnaise

½ cup dill pickles, chopped

1 tablespoon capers, rinsed and chopped

1 tablespoon green onions, chopped

1 tablespoon pickle juice

Kosher salt

Freshly ground black pepper

Corny's Crab Cakes with Tartar Sauce

Good morning, Baltimore! While vegetables are normally a good inclusion in a dish, for Maryland-inspired cakes, they are absolutely frowned upon. These Chesapeake Bay–style cakes have no filler veggies, allowing the sweetness of the lump crab meat to be the star. If you can, purchase crab that is refrigerated or fresh. Avoid the canned crab meat which can have additives that affect taste and texture.

With everything mixed together in one bowl, preparation is simple. The hardest part of this recipe will be the one hour wait time in the refrigerator. However impatient, don't skip this step. The time chilling and resting helps the flavors come together and will also help with shaping.

These crab meat patties fit the 1962 theme of Hairspray, *both in time period and location. Simple to form, these delicate cakes come together quickly—almost as fast as it takes to gobble them up.*

Place the crab meat into a large bowl and gently look over to remove loose pieces of crab shell. Add the mayonnaise, egg, lemon juice, Old Bay seasoning, Dijon mustard, Worcestershire sauce, and salt. Stir lightly to combine, then fold in the panko crumbs. Cover the bowl and refrigerate for at least one hour.

Divide the crab meat mixture into 8 round patties, about 2½ inches in diameter. In a nonstick skillet, heat about ¼ inch of oil over medium heat. Once the oil is hot, begin to fry the crab cakes. Cook a few at a time, being mindful to not overcrowd the pan.

Fry each patty for 3–4 minutes on each side, until the crust is golden brown. The crab cakes are delicate, so be gentle while flipping. Remove from pan and place to cool in a baking pan lined with paper towels or on a wire rack. Serve warm with lemon wedges and tartar sauce.

For Tartar Sauce

In a bowl, mix the mayonnaise, chopped pickles, capers, green onions, and pickle juice together. Season with salt and pepper. Cover and place in the refrigerator for 10 minutes to let rest and give the flavors a chance to blend together before serving.

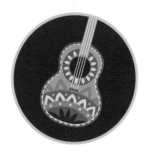

COCO
also *The Book of Life*
or *Into the Woods*

SERVES 6

¼ cup (½ stick) unsalted butter

3 cups fresh corn kernels
(cut from 2–3 ears)

2 cloves garlic, minced

½ cup mayonnaise

3 tablespoons minced
fresh cilantro

2–3 tablespoons fresh lime juice

¼ teaspoon chili powder

½ teaspoon Tajin seasoning

1 cup queso fresco (or Cotija or
feta cheese), plus more for garnish

½ teaspoon kosher salt

Freshly ground black pepper

Lime wedges for serving

Santa Cecilia Street Corn Cups

Called esquites or elote en vaso in Mexico, this corn-in-a-cup side dish is the epitome of street food. No street vendor in sight? Not a problem. You can make this from the comfort of your own kitchen.

Not wanting to strike up a grill, I tried to recreate the char effect by toasting the corn on a slightly higher heat. Mixed with creamy mayonnaise and salty crumbly cheese, this Mexican accompaniment will help bring in the festive spirit of Coco, The Book of Life, *or* Into the Woods.

On medium-high heat, melt the butter in a large skillet or cast-iron pan. Cook the corn, stirring occasionally, for 3–4 minutes. Add the garlic and cook for another 30 seconds. Remove from heat.

In a medium bowl, add the corn, mayonnaise, cilantro, lime juice, chili powder, Tajin seasoning, and queso fresco. Season to taste with salt and pepper. Scoop ½ cup corn into small containers or cups. Top with extra queso fresco and a lime wedge. Serve warm or at room temperature.

ACT I: Supporting Characters: Sides, Salads, and Dressings

44

MAKES 16 LATKES,
about 4 servings

Canola oil for frying

2 eggs

⅓ cup all-purpose flour

1 tablespoon matzo meal
or breadcrumbs

1 teaspoon baking powder

2 teaspoons kosher salt

Freshly ground black pepper

1 (20-ounce) bag frozen shredded
hash browns, thawed

1 cup grated onions

Sour cream, for serving

Sliced green onions, for serving

Applesauce, for serving

Anatevka Potato Latkes

A Jewish potato pancake, these latkes are made with the use of frozen hash browns. The latkes are crispy-crunchy fried on the outside, with a creamy potato and onion filling on the inside. Mainly prepared to celebrate Hanukkah, an eight-day Jewish festival, these latkes can be used for a watching of Fiddler on the Roof.

In a large skillet, heat about ½-inch of oil over medium heat. Line a half-sheet baking pan with paper towels or set a wire rack inside the pan.

In a large bowl, beat the eggs. Next mix in the flour, matzo meal or breadcrumbs, baking powder, salt, and pepper. Mix in thawed, shredded hash browns and onions and form into 1½-inch balls. Flatten into patties about ½-inch thick.

Add the latkes to the heated oil in the skillet. Fry until golden brown in color, about 2–4 minutes on each side. Remove and drain on paper towels or cooling rack. Serve warm, topped with sour cream and green onions or applesauce.

SERVES 6

4 tablespoons (½ stick) unsalted butter

1 cup chopped yellow onion (about 1 medium onion)

2 cloves garlic, minced

1 teaspoon kosher salt, divided

⅓ cup all-purpose flour

6 cups chicken broth

4 cups (1 head) chopped cauliflower

½ cup heavy cream

Salt and pepper to taste

1 (16-ounce) package bacon, cooked and crumbled

1 cup roasted hazelnuts, chopped

Flat leaf parsley (optional)

Garden Envy Cauliflower Soup with Hazelnuts

Evil fake mothers aside, Rapunzel's Mother Gothel knew something about the comfort of soup. Soup is one of Cassius's favorite meals, especially if the creamy vegetable base is finished off with savory toppings like salty bacon and rich hazelnuts. If you don't have an immersion blender, you can also use a food processor or blender to make this soup smooth. Allow the soup to cool for 20 minutes or so before blending, and fill the blender in half-full batches to avoid splatters.

Waiting for the soup to cool down before mixing requires some patience, but it will be worth it. Pureed together, the soup becomes creamy and rich. Kids may forget the main ingredient is cauliflower. It's so good, you don't even need to lock anyone in a tower to eat it.

In a large soup pot or Dutch oven, melt the unsalted butter over medium heat. Add the chopped onions and sauté for 6–8 minutes until softened, stirring frequently with a wooden spoon. Add the minced garlic and ½ teaspoon of salt. Continue to stir for about 30 seconds. This will allow the garlic to become fragrant.

Add the flour, stirring constantly with a whisk for about one minute. The flour will begin to turn golden brown, about the color of butterscotch. The mixture will also thicken, making a roux. Slowly add the broth to the pot, continuing to whisk broth into the roux.

Add the chopped cauliflower and let it simmer over medium heat for 30–35 minutes until the soup is a bit bubbly and the vegetables soft. With an immersion blender, blend the soup in the pot. If you're using a blender or food processor, allow the soup to cool for about 20 minutes before mixing.

Once smooth, add cream, then salt and pepper to taste. Reheat the soup. Ladle the soup into bowls and sprinkle with crispy bacon pieces, chopped hazelnuts, and (optional) chopped flat leaf parsley.

MAKES ONE 13x18
HALF-SHEET PAN

Nonstick baking spray

2 pounds (about 3 medium)
sweet potatoes

3 tablespoons canola oil

1 tablespoon berbere spice blend

2 cloves garlic, grated or minced

1 teaspoon kosher salt

Hakuna Yamatata Berbere Fries

The young warthogs in my house love all things fries. These sweet potato fries are baked in the oven and seasoned with berbere, a warm spice blend featuring fenugreek and cardamom. This seasoning is peppery and vibrant. Almost giving off a BBQ vibe, it's a little spicy with some tang.

The sweet potato fries are a great side dish for a viewing of The Lion King. *Don't know what else to do with the bottle of berbere you bought for this recipe? No worries! This spice is incredibly versatile. Sprinkle over meat or vegetables, and it may become your next kitchen staple— and not just a passing craze.*

Preheat oven to 425 degrees F. and set rack in the center. Spray a 13x18 half-sheet baking pan with cooking spray. While the oven heats up, pop in the half-sheet pan. Warming up the pan will help the sweet potatoes not stick.

Peel and cut the sweet potatoes into 2-inch wedges or fries. In a large bowl, toss the sweet potatoes, oil, berbere spice, grated garlic, and salt. Remove the warmed pan from the oven and place the seasoned sweet potatoes on the greased pan and roast 30–40 minutes. Potatoes will be browned and soft when pricked with a fork. Serve hot.

ACT I: Supporting Characters: Sides, Salads, and Dressings

DARBY O'GILL AND THE LITTLE PEOPLE
also *Song of the Sea*

SERVES 6–8

2 pounds new or small
red potatoes, scrubbed

½ cup (1 stick) unsalted butter

¼ cup water

1 teaspoon kosher salt

½ teaspoon freshly
ground black pepper

¼ cup chopped parsley, optional

King Brian's Butter Boiled Potatoes

I spent many summers in small-town Idaho visiting family, and you can say my love for potatoes runs deep. When Norma, my mother-in-law, made these simple butter boiled potatoes for St. Patrick's Day, I knew this recipe would become a family favorite. Steamed in a mixture of butter and water, these potatoes become fluffy and soft.

This side dish is a great accompaniment for any Irish-influenced musical, like a classic St. Patrick's Day watching of Darby O'Gill and the Little People *or the animated* Song of the Sea.

Remove a small section of peel from each potato with a vegetable peeler—one strip along the side or bottom of the potato will do. Set potatoes aside.

In a large pot, melt butter over medium-low heat. Add the water, salt, and pepper to the pool of melted butter. Place potatoes in the pot. Cover with pot lid and cook for 20–30 minutes, rolling the potatoes around in the pan occasionally to keep them from sticking. Avoid removing the lid to keep steam in.

The potatoes are finished when fork-tender. Transfer to a large serving bowl and sprinkle with chopped parsley. Drizzle the remaining butter mixture from the pot over the potatoes and season to taste with salt and pepper. If desired, top with optional chopped parsley.

**BEAUTY AND
THE BEAST**

MAKES 1 CUP

3 tablespoons fresh lemon juice

1 tablespoon white wine vinegar

Zest from 1 lemon

1 tablespoon Dijon mustard

2–3 teaspoons granulated sugar

¼ teaspoon kosher salt

¾ cup extra-virgin olive oil

Castle Feast Lemon Vinaigrette

An everyday vinaigrette, this French-inspired dressing is light and tangy. The Dijon mustard helps emulsify and give creaminess. The sugar brings out the sweetness of the lemons.

Set in France, Beauty and Beast *would be a good musical for salads topped with this dressing.*

Whisk together the lemon juice, white wine vinegar, lemon zest, Dijon mustard, 2 teaspoons of sugar, and salt. Add more sugar to taste. Continue to whisk, slowly drizzling in the olive oil until emulsified.

LILO & STITCH
also *Moana*

SERVES 12–15
AS A SIDE

3 teaspoons kosher salt

1 (16-ounce) package
elbow macaroni

1 medium carrot

1 small onion

2 cups mayonnaise

3-4 tablespoons dill pickle juice

½ teaspoon freshly ground pepper

Hawaiian Mac Salad

There are many variations of Hawaiian-style macaroni salad. Some make it mixed with chunks of tuna or chopped eggs. Others prefer olives, with the addition of soft potatoes and crunchy celery. I like mine rather simple—onions so fine they disappear into the salty mayo mixture, carrots grated into tiny slivers, and of course big soft noodles.

Keep this elbow-shaped pasta cooking for a few minutes longer than you're used to, until the noodles are soft and slightly bloated—almost to the point of overcooked. No al dente rules here.

Sitting next to a plate of grilled meats, mac salad is a great accompaniment to any picnic or outdoor function or a watching of Lilo & Stitch *or* Moana. *If you're stuck on the mainland like me, this little scoop of Hawaii is like having the islands on your plate. You're welcome.*

Fill a large pot with water. Add salt and boil water on medium heat. Once the water comes to a rolling boil, add the dry macaroni. Forget everything you know about perfectly cooked pasta and boil the noodles until they are soft and over-cooked, but not falling apart, about 15 minutes. Drain and rinse the noodles under cold water. Transfer to a large bowl.

While the pasta is cooking, peel the carrot and cut off the ends. Using a grater, shred the carrot until you get about ½ cup. Set aside. Peel off onion skin. Using the small holes on a box grater or a microplane grater, grate the onion. The grated onion should resemble a paste with the onion juices mixed with the pulp. Grate the onion until you've collected ¼ cup.

In a medium bowl, add the mayonnaise, ¼ cup grated onion, and pickle juice and mix together. Pour the mixture over the cooked macaroni and stir. Toss in the grated carrots and mix. Season with salt and pepper to taste. Cover the bowl with plastic wrap and refrigerate for at least 1 hour before serving.

HERCULES

SERVES 6

4 large (about 2 pounds) russet potatoes, scrubbed

Olive oil

½ teaspoon kosher salt

Freshly ground black pepper

1 tablespoon fresh oregano, finely chopped (or 1 teaspoon dried)

¼ teaspoon garlic powder

Zest of 1 medium lemon (about 1 tablespoon)

½ cup feta cheese, crumbled

Lemon juice from 1 medium lemon (about 2-3 tablespoons)

Going the Distance
Feta Cheese Fries

Salty feta cheese and rich olive oil take these oven-baked fries up a level—almost to the top of Mount Olympus. Soaking the fries in cold water helps remove starch and bake up crispy. Soft potatoes are surrounded by a crisp exterior and are so good you won't miss the frying in oil. Kosher salt and lemon juice give the potato slices a tangy flavor.

These fries are flavorful enough on their own, but also good dipped in The Muses' Cucumber Yogurt Tzatziki (see recipe on page 76).

Cut potatoes into fries about ¼ inch thick. Keep the skins on for added texture. Fill a large bowl with ice water and soak the cut potatoes for 30 minutes to an hour. Remove fries and pat dry with a kitchen towel.

Preheat oven to 450 degrees F. and place rack in center. Coat two rimmed half-sheet baking pans with oil and place in the oven. As your oven heats, the baking pans will also. The hot pans will help the fries not stick to them.

In a large bowl, toss the fries with 1 tablespoon of olive oil, salt, pepper, oregano, garlic powder, and lemon zest. Remove the heated pans from the oven and add the seasoned fries in a single layer.

Roast for 25–30 minutes, flipping the fries about halfway. Sprinkle the crumbled feta cheese over the fries then cook for 5 more minutes, giving the cheese time to melt just a little. Remove from oven, sprinkle with some or all of the lemon juice, adjusted to taste. Serve hot.

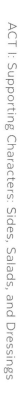

ACT I: Supporting Characters: Sides, Salads, and Dressings

THE LITTLE MERMAID
also *Beauty and the Beast*

SERVES 4–6

2 cups or ½ pound small yellow or red potatoes, cut into large chunks or quarters

½ pound small new potatoes, halved

1 tablespoon salt

2 cups or ½ pound fresh green beans, such as haricots verts, trimmed

2 cups grape or cherry tomatoes, sliced in half

2 cups English cucumbers, sliced

3 cans oil-packed tuna or 3 cups shredded cooked chicken

½ cup olives, capers, or pickles

6 hardboiled eggs, peeled and halved

1 head iceberg lettuce

Kosher salt and freshly ground black pepper to taste

1 batch of Castle Feast Lemon Vinaigrette (see recipe on page 55)

Triton's Salade Niçoise

This French salad is great as a side or even as a meal on a warm day. Most of the work is spent in assembly by blanching—or quick boiling—the vegetables. Haricots verts, or slender crispy green beans, are a niçoise salad staple, and this all can be made ahead of time.

With the addition of tuna, it goes well with a viewing of **The Little Mermaid.** *The French countryside of* **Beauty and the Beast** *could also be represented by substituting shredded chicken for tuna.*

Place the potatoes in a large pot and cover with cold water. Add 1 tablespoon salt. On medium heat, bring to a boil. Once boiling, reduce heat to medium-low and cook for 10-15 minutes or until potatoes are soft enough to pierce with a fork. Remove and drain potatoes.

To blanch the green beans, using the same pot or a new one, bring a large pot of salted water to a boil over medium heat. Add the green beans and cook for 2-3 minutes, until tender and bright green. Drain beans and transfer to a bowl of ice water about 4-6 minutes. Remove cooled beans from water and set aside.

On a large platter, arrange the salad. Use iceberg lettuce leaves as a base. Place the cooked potatoes, green beans, tomatoes, cucumbers, and tuna or chicken into groupings around the dish. Add the olives, capers, or pickles on top and layer the hardboiled eggs around the vegetables. Sprinkle with salt and pepper to taste and serve with Castle Feast Lemon Vinaigrette (see recipe on page 55).

ACT I: Supporting Characters: Sides, Salads, and Dressings

MAKES 2½–3 CUPS
OF BEANS

Canola oil for cooking

½ cup onions, finely chopped

½ teaspoon kosher salt

¼ teaspoon black pepper

1 cup water

1 tablespoon apple cider vinegar

1 tablespoon tomato paste

½ teaspoon Worcestershire sauce

1 tablespoon yellow mustard

1 tablespoon maple
syrup or brown sugar

2 teaspoons blackstrap molasses

2 teaspoon garlic powder

2 (15-ounce) cans white beans
(such as navy, cannellini,
or Great Northern beans),
drained and rinsed

You'll Be Back
British Baked Beans

More savory than their American baked bean counterparts, British baked beans have a unique tang. No smokey meat or sweet brown sugar here, these tomato-based beans are also a must in a full English breakfast, such as Henry Higgins's Proper Full English on page 15. On toast for a light lunch, these beans would also work well for a viewing of Hamilton, Mary Poppins, *or* Matilda.

Heat a large pot or Dutch oven over medium heat. Add oil to coat the bottom and sauté the chopped onions with salt and pepper. Stir constantly with a wooden spoon until onions are soft and brown at edges, about 5–8 minutes.

Add the water, apple cider vinegar, tomato paste, Worcestershire sauce, yellow mustard, maple syrup, molasses, and garlic powder. Stir again to combine. Whisk if needed to break up any clumps. Increase the heat to medium-high and add the rinsed beans. Stir for 6–8 minutes, giving the sauce time to reduce. Salt and pepper to taste. Serve warm.

INTERMISSION

Stretch your legs after a long Act I and take a break with
some of these dishes. Of course, these snacks can be served
and eaten anytime, not just at the midpoint of the musical.

Snacks

Creamy Dreamy Hummus
Hercules 67

San Ángel Guacamole
The Book of Life 68

The March Hare's Deviled Eggs
Alice in Wonderland 71

Red Panda Angry Edamame
Turning Red 72

Fried Wonton Moons
Mulan 75

The Muses' Cucumber Yogurt Tzatziki
Hercules 76

Phil's Peppermint Pretzel Bark
White Christmas 79

Ringmaster Kettle Corn
The Greatest Showman 80

Beverages

Pink Lady Lemonade
Grease 83

SkyDome Strawberry Milk
Turning Red 84

Christmas Town Hot Cocoa Mix
The Nightmare Before Christmas 87

T-Birds' Rockin'
Chocolate Cherry Cola Float
Grease 88

Warm Hugs Frozen Cocoa
Frozen 91

Club Car
Malted Milkshakes
White Christmas 92

MAKES 2 CUPS

1 (15-ounce) can chickpeas, drained and rinsed

½ teaspoon baking soda

¼ cup tahini

3 tablespoons lemon juice

¼ cup extra-virgin olive oil

½ teaspoon garlic powder

½ teaspoon ground cumin

¾ teaspoon kosher salt

2–4 tablespoons ice water, more as needed

Creamy Dreamy Hummus

Smooth and creamy with bright notes of lemon and savory garlic, homemade hummus is a great accompaniment to many Mediterranean dishes. It's also commonly found in Greek restaurants alongside staples like flatbreads and can also be included in a Jewish menu—a great appetizer for both Hercules *and* Fiddler on the Roof.

After a twenty-minute boil with baking soda, canned chickpeas are soft and ready to mash. This recipe comes together fairly fast in a food processor.

In a medium saucepan over medium heat, add the drained and rinsed chickpeas, cover with water, and add baking soda. Bring to a boil and cook until soft and the outer skins of the chickpeas begin to fall off, about 20 minutes. Drain and rinse with cool water.

In a food processor, add the soft chickpeas, tahini, lemon juice, olive oil, garlic powder, cumin, salt, and ice water. Process until smooth, about 30 seconds to 1 minute, adding more water if needed for texture. Transfer to a serving bowl and chill for 30 minutes, allowing time for the flavors to blend. Before serving, drizzle with additional olive oil. Serve cold.

THE BOOK OF LIFE
also *Coco*

MAKES 3 CUPS,
ABOUT 4–6 SERVINGS

3 ripe large Hass avocados

½ cup minced white onion

1 clove garlic, minced

1 Roma tomato, chopped

½ cup chopped fresh cilantro

1–2 tablespoons finely
chopped jalapeño, seeded
(optional to lessen heat)

3 tablespoons fresh lime juice

Kosher salt

San Ángel Guacamole

From tacos to toast, guacamole is a creamy fixture at our home. My tip is to lightly mash the avocado while stirring. I prefer guacamole a little chunky and not super smooth. I also season pretty liberally with salt, adding just enough lime juice to brighten but not overpower.

Serve this side dish with tortilla chips for an appetizer while watching The Book of Life *or* Coco. *Guacamole can also make a quick breakfast spread on a slice of bread or toast.*

Pit, scoop, and cut the avocados into a large bowl and smash with a potato masher. Add the onions, minced garlic, chopped tomatoes, cilantro, and jalapeño and stir gently until well incorporated. Season with lime juice and salt to taste. Serve immediately and refrigerate leftovers.

MAKES 12
DEVILED EGGS

6 hard-boiled large eggs,
chilled and peeled

3 tablespoons mayonnaise

1 teaspoon Dijon mustard

1 teaspoon dill pickle juice

⅛ teaspoon Tabasco sauce

Kosher salt and freshly ground
black pepper to taste

Ground paprika

Chopped chives

Sliced olives (optional)

The March Hare's Deviled Eggs

A party staple for potlucks and other gatherings, this appetizer will be great for an Alice in Wonderland *tea party or retro viewings of* That Thing You Do. *Topped with a sliced olive to take on the appearance of an eyeball, deviled eggs can also be spooky appetizers for* The Nightmare Before Christmas.

A trick I learned for assembling deviled eggs is to use a very cold knife when slicing hard-boiled eggs. Running the knife under cold water will do the trick. The cold helps to make a clean cut. Filled with creamy yolk, these bite-sized hors d'oeuvres are always welcome at our table.

Rinse a sharp knife under cold water. Using the cold knife, slice each egg in half lengthwise. Remove the egg yolks and add to a bowl. Set egg whites aside. Mash the egg yolks and stir in mayonnaise, Dijon mustard, pickle juice, and Tabasco sauce. Add salt and pepper to taste.

Using a pastry bag or spoon, fill each egg white half with the smooth yolk filling. Sprinkle with ground paprika and chopped chives. For a spooky eyeball appearance, add an olive slice.

TURNING RED

SERVES 2-4

8 ounces frozen edamame
in shell, about 1½ cups

2 tablespoons + 1 teaspoon
kosher salt, divided

½–1 teaspoon shichimi
togarashi seasoning

Orange zest

Red Panda Angry Edamame

We first discovered this spicy—or "angry"—edamame dish at a Japanese-Hawaiian restaurant ages ago. It was ordered as an appetizer, and the genius of sprinkling shichimi togarashi—a Japanese spice blend of red chili, sesame seeds, nori, dried orange peel, ground ginger, and poppy seeds—over the soybean pods made quite an impression. Years later, I can hardly recall anything else we ordered that night. Yet I still remember this delicious soybean snack, bright and citrusy with a peppery kick.

If you live near an Asian market, picking up a bottle of shichimi togarashi shouldn't be a problem. It's also easily found online. This is a worthwhile snack for some of the Asian themed musicals like Turning Red.

Add frozen edamame to a microwave-safe bowl and cover with water. Add 2 tablespoons of salt and microwave for 6 minutes. Allow to cool and drain water. Add drained edamame to another bowl, and toss with 1 teaspoon of kosher salt, ½ to 1 teaspoon of shichimi togarashi seasoning and a pinch or a few grates of orange zest. Serve warm or at room temperature.

72

MULAN
also *Turning Red*

MAKES 40–50 WONTONS

¾ pound ground pork

1 tablespoon garlic, minced

2 tablespoons grated ginger, peeled

3 tablespoons sliced green onions

½ cup carrots, minced

1 egg, beaten

1 tablespoon soy sauce

1 tablespoon rice wine or rice wine vinegar

1 tablespoon sesame oil

1 tablespoon cornstarch

¼ teaspoon crushed red peppers

1 package wonton wrappers

1–2 cups water

Canola oil for frying, about 2 cups

Sweet chili sauce (optional)

Fried Wonton Moons

I make wontons the same way that my mom did—in simple triangles that, once tucked, take on the shape of crescent moons.

This is not a conventional way to wrap a wonton, but I actually like the extra crunch of the wrapper in triangle shape and have taught my kids to fold wontons the same. The addition of carrots is another thing passed on by Mom. Sneaking in vegetables along with lazy wonton wrapping runs in the family.

While preparing the filling takes a little time in the kitchen, the assembly is something the whole family can do. You can start prepping while watching Turning Red *or* Mulan.

Mix all ingredients—except wonton wrappers, water, canola oil, and sweet chili sauce—together and refrigerate for at least 30 minutes. To assemble, place a few wonton wrappers on a clean working surface like a large cutting board. Lay a damp paper towel over the remaining wrappers to keep them from drying out. Fill a small bowl of water for sealing the wontons. Place one teaspoon of filling in the center of one wonton wrapper. With your fingertips, wet the edges of the wrapper with water. Fold over into a triangle shape and seal together like an envelope, pressing out excess air. Fill all wontons and place on a separate surface, being careful not to overlap to avoid them sticking together.

Meanwhile, heat about 3 inches of oil in a large pot on medium heat. When oil is hot (around 375 degrees), fry wontons until golden brown, about three to five minutes each. Remove from oil and place on a wire rack to cool. Repeat with all wontons. Serve immediately plain or with sweet chili sauce.

MAKES 2–2½ CUPS

½ cup finely grated
English cucumber, excess
water squeezed out

2 cups full-fat Greek yogurt

2 tablespoons fresh lemon juice

1 tablespoon extra-virgin olive oil

½ teaspoon garlic powder

1 tablespoon chopped fresh dill
(or 2 teaspoons dried dill)

1 teaspoon kosher salt

The Muses' Cucumber Yogurt Tzatziki

This yogurt and cucumber dip is bright from the lemon juice and just a bit tart from the yogurt. Traditionally made with sheep or goat yogurt—which can be hard to find—using full-fat Greek yogurt makes this dip accessible with an everyday grocery store run.

Serve with slices of warm pita bread, grilled vegetables, and Greek-style meatballs for a meal fit for Hercules or maybe even his father, Zeus.

In a medium bowl, mix together the grated and strained cucumber, yogurt, fresh lemon juice, olive oil, garlic powder, dill, and salt. Serve cold.

MAKES 1 LARGE BAKING SHEET OF BARK

1 (12-ounce) package semisweet chocolate chips

½ teaspoon peppermint extract

3 cups of broken-up pretzels (I use smaller pretzels, like sticks or mini twists)

16 ounces white chocolate chips or vanilla bark

½ teaspoon peppermint extract

3–4 candy canes, smashed into ¼ cup

Phil's Peppermint Pretzel Bark

I believe in the gift of giving neighborhood cookie plates during the holidays. Baking and assembling these homemade gifts during the busiest month of the year is peak stressful—but also rewarding.

One of the treats that goes on the Bybee yearly plate is this minty, chocolatey, salty peppermint pretzel bark. The dusting of smashed candy canes signals Christmastime, and the addition of salty pretzels cuts through the rich sweetness of the chocolate. They are a good addition to the cookie plate, but also something that can last for a couple of weeks on the counter.

Line a 9x13 pan with parchment paper.

In a microwave-safe bowl, melt the chocolate chips in the microwave in 30-second intervals. Once they begin to melt, give them a stir; more chips will melt once stirred. Add ½ teaspoon of peppermint extract and mix in.

Using a rubber spatula or flat spatula, spread the melted chocolate on the prepared 9x13 pan. Press in the broken-up pretzels, carefully pushing the pretzels into the chocolate. Let cool until chocolate is hardened.

In a separate microwave-safe bowl, melt the white chocolate for about 1–2 minutes in 30 second intervals. Once melted, mix in ½ teaspoon peppermint extract. Carefully pour the peppermint white chocolate over the chocolate and pretzel layer. Spread quickly and top with crushed candy canes. Allow to cool until the bark hardens. On a clean work surface, such as a clean cutting board, cut into pieces with a large chef's knife.

¼ cup canola oil

½ cup popcorn kernels

¼ cup granulated sugar

1 teaspoon kosher salt

Ringmaster Kettle Corn

To me, one of the greatest creations in popcorn history is the invention of the Whirley Pop. It helps distribute oil (and sugar in this kettle corn recipe) to each kernel, which makes for minimal to no burning. This stovetop popcorn maker has a handle to help stir the popcorn as it cooks. It makes theater-ready popcorn in about three minutes, enough for the entire family. However, if you don't have this popcorn maker, cooking in a large pot will also work.

A big bowl of kettle corn is an essential ticket to fun and feeling young at a state fair—also for watching The Greatest Showman.

On medium heat, heat oil in a Whirley Pop or large covered pot. Add popcorn kernels and whirl or shake the covered pot. As soon as the kernels start to pop, add in the sugar and crank the Whirly Pop handle. If using a pot, wait one minute for the sugar to start melting. Open the lid and give the sugar and kernels a quick stir with a wooden spoon. With the Whirley Pop or pot, continue to stir until the kernels stop popping, about three minutes.

Remove from heat and transfer popcorn to a large bowl. Sprinkle salt over popcorn, tossing to combine and separate. Serve immediately.

**MAKES 5 CUPS OF
LEMONADE SYRUP**

1 cup water

3 cups granulated sugar

3 cups lemon juice
(juice of 16–18 lemons)

2–3 tablespoons lemon zest
(zest of 3 lemons)

Grenadine syrup

Pink Lady Lemonade

A little bit sour, a tiny smidge sweet, this lemonade gives homage to the pink ladies of Rydell High. A simple lemon syrup that can be used to make lemonade, it can be stored in the fridge for anytime (greased) lightning strikes. Mix the syrup with water and a splash of grenadine that gives it its trademark pink color. Lemonade is also served in White Christmas, *so it works for this musical too.*

In a large pot, add 1 cup of water and boil on medium-high heat. Once the water comes to a boil, add the sugar, lemon juice, and lemon zest.

Turn heat to medium. As the sugar breaks down, it will become a syrup. Cook until sugar is dissolved, about 3–5 minutes. You can store the syrup in the refrigerator or use right away.

To make a glass of lemonade, mix ¼ cup syrup in 1 cup of water. Add a few drops of grenadine for color and stir.

TURNING RED
also *Alice in Wonderland*

MAKES ABOUT
2¾ CUPS OF PUREE

Strawberry Puree

1 lb. fresh strawberries,
preferably overripe

½ cup granulated sugar

1 teaspoon salt

Milk for serving

SkyDome Strawberry Milk

This recipe is from Brendan, who, like a good dad, came up with this pink milk concoction for a birthday tea party so many years ago. Use your ugly, bruised, and overripe strawberries here. The more banged up they are, the greater the strawberry milk will be. Older berries that hover around almost bad are the easiest to break down for the strawberry puree.

With the strawberries, this milk is very light pink in color, but still falling in the red color spectrum, so maybe it's a bit of a stretch to enjoy while watching Turning Red. *I still think it fits. You can also serve this in cute teapots for a tea party, and this sweet, fruity-flavored milk will make any* Alice in Wonderland *party that much more delicious.*

Remove green stems and place strawberries, sugar, salt, and a tablespoon of water into a blender. Blend on high until smooth, adding water in tablespoons as needed to puree the berries. If you don't have a particularly powerful blender, allow the fruit and sugar to macerate, or soften, for about 30 minutes. This will help the strawberries break down and blend easier. Mix 4 tablespoons of strawberry puree for 8 ounces (or one tall glass) of milk. Serve cold.

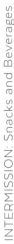

INTERMISSION: Snacks and Beverages

SERVES 8

1 cup confectioners' sugar

½ cup Dutch-processed
cocoa powder

¾ cup powdered milk

2 teaspoons cornstarch

½ cup mini chocolate chips

½ teaspoon kosher salt

Christmas Town Hot Cocoa Mix

Keeping this homemade hot cocoa mix on hand will ensure many cozy evenings of watching holiday films like The Nightmare Before Christmas. *The confectioners' sugar helps the cocoa mix melt easily, and the mini chocolate chips amp up the flavor (and fun). Serve in a teapot, and it can also be used for a great* Alice in Wonderland *hot chocolate tea party.*

In a large bowl, whisk together the confectioners' sugar, cocoa powder, powdered milk, cornstarch, mini chocolate chips, and salt. Store in an airtight container with lid. To use, mix ⅓ cup of cocoa mix to 1 cup of hot water and stir.

GREASE
also *The Greatest Showman*

MAKES 1 FLOAT

1 cup cold cherry cola, such as Cherry Coke

1 teaspoon grenadine syrup

2 tablespoons Showstopper Hot Fudge Sauce, divided (see recipe on page 159)

2 scoops (about 1 cup) chocolate ice cream

Big Top Whipped Cream (see recipe on page 160)

Maraschino cherries for garnish

T-Birds' Rockin' Chocolate Cherry Cola Float

I would like to bring back the soda shop drinks of the 1950s, please, where scoops of ice cream mingle with fizzy carbonated soda and create a blissful pairing of cream and carbonation. Served with a side of fries and a burger, these T-Birds' Rockin' Chocolate Cherry Cola Floats also make the menu in Grease.

While grenadine is made from pomegranates, not cherries, the sweet and tart flavor makes the cherry cola fruitier and gives it a slightly reddish tinge. These chocolate floats would also be good for a refreshing carnival drink while watching The Greatest Showman.

Mix the cherry cola and grenadine syrup in a large container such as a tall mason jar or 16-ounce water bottle. Set aside.

Add 1 tablespoon of hot fudge sauce to the bottom of a tall glass. Add 2 scoops of chocolate ice cream. Slowly pour the cherry cola/grenadine mixture into the glass. Top with whipped cream, 1 tablespoon hot fudge, and a maraschino cherry.

2 cups chocolate milk

½ cup Christmas Town Hot Cocoa
Mix (see recipe on page 87)

1 frozen banana

1 cup ice

Optional Toppings

Big Top Whipped Cream
(see recipe on page 160)

Showstopper Hot Fudge Sauce
(see recipe on page 159)

Chocolate shavings

Chocolate sprinkles

Warm Hugs Frozen Cocoa

Thicker than chocolate milk but not as decadent as a milkshake, frozen hot chocolate exists somewhere in the overlapping Venn diagram of these beverages. The frozen banana is the trick here, giving the drink extra bulk. (Also a great way to sneak in secret fruit for the kids!) While this frozen cocoa is frosty and cold, it's also comforting like a warm hug in the winter. Break out chilled glasses and fill them to the brim for a watching of Frozen.

In a blender, blend the chocolate milk, hot cocoa mix, frozen banana, and ice until smooth. Pour into two glasses and top with whipped cream, hot fudge, or chocolate shavings or sprinkles.

WHITE CHRISTMAS
also *Grease*

SERVES 2

2 scoops (about 1 cup)
chocolate ice cream

1 cup milk

½ cup malted milk balls,
such as Whoppers

1–2 tablespoons malt
powder (optional)

For Serving

1 tablespoon chocolate syrup
or Showstopper Hot Fudge
Sauce (see recipe on page 159)

Big Top Whipped Cream
(see recipe on page 160)

Crushed malted milk balls,
such as Whoppers

Chocolate sprinkles (optional)

Club Car
Malted Milkshakes

In my desire to bring back the retro desserts of yore, I stumbled across the mention of a malted milkshake in White Christmas*—this holiday musical is chock full of food references! Malted milkshakes are also on the menu at the Frosty Palace, the 1950s diner in* Grease*. Creamy chocolate ice cream blended with malted milk balls and malt powder and served in a frosty glass? I'm dreaming of a* White Christmas *viewing with this old-fashioned milkshake!*

In my vintage rendition, this chocolate malt milkshake is also a nod to a Thrifty ice cream flavor, Chocolate Malted Krunch. Thrifty was a Southern California ice cream institution sold in drugstores that also became popular along the West Coast. Note: malt powder may be hard to find. Look for it in the baking section of the grocery stores. I've had success finding some at big-box discount retailers, such as Target or Walmart.

Place the ice cream, milk, and malted milk balls in a blender. Blend on lowest speed to just combine. Increase to medium speed and blend until smooth, about one minute. If you want a stronger malt flavor, add in the optional malt powder.

Scoop 1 tablespoon hot fudge in the bottom of tall, chilled glasses. Pour in milkshake and top with whipped cream, chopped malted milk balls, or other toppings.

ACT II

In musicals, Act II is where the meat of the story happens. Get your fill with these hearty main course dishes.

Entrees

Emerald Isle Shepherd's Pie
Song of the Sea 97

Under the Californian Sea Sushi Rolls
The Little Mermaid 98

Lunchtime Spam Musubi
Lilo & Stitch 101

Kalua Pulled Pork
Lilo & Stitch 102

Edna's Crispy Chicken Cutlets
Hairspray 105

Fat Sam's Grand Slam Chicken Parmesan
Bugsy Malone 106

Boat Snack Loco Moco
Moana 109

Hermes's Greek Meatballs
Hercules 110

Jade Rabbit's
Honey Soy Glazed Chicken
Over the Moon 113

Polar Turkey Burgers
Grease 114

Von Trapp Schnitzel
with Noodles
The Sound of Music . . . 117

Selkie's Secret Pan-Fried Fish
Song of the Sea 118

Uncle Albert Bubble
and Squeak Patties
Mary Poppins 121

We Finish Each Other's
Turkey, Ham, and Bacon
Club Sandwiches
Frozen 122

SERVES 20

Canola oil for cooking

2 pounds ground beef,
pork, and/or lamb

1 cup onions, chopped

2 cups (about 2 large)
carrots, chopped

1 cup (about 2 ribs) celery, chopped

2 cloves garlic, minced

1 sprig fresh thyme

3 tablespoons all-purpose flour

2 tablespoons tomato paste

1 (14.5 ounce) can beef broth

1 tablespoon Worcestershire sauce

Salt and pepper, to taste

1 cup frozen peas

6 cups mashed potatoes,
warm (see Bob Cratchit's
Smooth Mashed Potatoes
recipe on page 39)

½ cup sour cream

½ cup Parmesan cheese

1 egg, beaten

Emerald Isle Shepherd's Pie

Shepherd's Pie has roots in Scotland, England, and Ireland. It was the Irish who started using potatoes instead of a pastry topping to repurpose leftovers. A mixture of ground meat and vegetables is topped with a layer of thick mashed potatoes. Baked in a 9x13 pan, this hearty meat pie casserole serves a crowd. We like to swirl our potatoes with a fork to resemble ocean waves, a great effect for a viewing of Song of the Sea.

Preheat oven to 400 degrees F. Move rack to the middle of the oven.

In a cast-iron pan or large skillet over medium heat, heat just enough oil to coat the bottom. Brown the ground meat. Cook, stirring occasionally, about 6–8 minutes. Drain excess fat or liquid and add chopped onions, carrots, and celery. Cook the vegetables until soft, about 4–6 minutes. Add garlic and thyme and continue to cook, about 3–5 minutes.

Stir in flour, tomato paste, beef broth, and Worcestershire sauce. As the mixture cooks, it will thicken. Reduce heat to medium-low and cook about 7–10 minutes. Season with salt and pepper to taste. Add in peas. Remove from heat and spread evenly into a 9x13 baking pan.

In a large bowl, stir together the warm mashed potatoes, sour cream, and Parmesan cheese. Top the ground meat and vegetables in the baking pan with the mashed potato mixture. Brush the beaten egg over the mashed potatoes.

Bake in oven for 30–40 minutes, or until the potatoes are golden brown and bubbly at the edges. Serve hot.

THE LITTLE MERMAID

SERVES 8

6 cups cooked sushi or
short-grain rice, such as Calrose

½ cup seasoned rice vinegar

Crab Mixture

1 (10-ounce) package imitation
crab meat, separated and flaked

⅓ cup mayonnaise

8 half-sheets nori

1 English cucumber, cut
into thin strips

1 avocado, sliced thin

Under the Californian Sea Sushi Rolls

These California rolls are fun to make with the family but hardly ever turn out pretty—at least in our house. It's some work to prep the ingredients, but gathering together around the table to assemble is a rewarding activity.

My number one tip is to not expect the sushi rolls to come out perfectly on the first try. Or second, or third. It takes some practice to not overstuff or under stuff the rolls. If making with kids, help the little ones with the construction by giving the finished rolls a firm squeeze in the rolling mats. They will also need adult help with slicing the rolls into pieces.

In a large bowl, add the cooked rice and rice vinegar. Stir and fan the rice until it cools to room temperature. Set aside. In a medium bowl, mix the flaked imitation crab with the mayo. Set aside.

Cover a rolling mat or thick straw placemat with plastic wrap. This will help the rice not stick to the mat. Place one nori sheet on the rolling mat, the rough side of the seaweed facing up. With wet hands, scoop up enough rice to make a small ball about three inches across. Spread the rice across the entire nori square. Flip the nori so the rice is touching the plastic wrap and the seaweed is facing up. Place a spoonful of crab mixture along a horizontal row in the middle of the nori. Top this line with cucumbers and avocado.

Picking up the mat on one side, roll it over the crab filling to make a long cylinder. Give the roll a squeeze as you press the rice together. Place on a cutting board and, with a sharp, wet knife, slice into 6 pieces. Serve immediately.

SERVES 8

1 (12-ounce) tin canned
meat, such as Spam

2 tablespoons soy sauce

2 tablespoons granulated sugar

2 cups cooked white,
short-grain rice

4 nori sheets split into thirds

Lunchtime Spam Musubi

Sold individually in plastic wrap, Spam musubi can be found at the counters of Hawaiian convenience stores for a snack or a quick lunch. At my house, it's Mei's fallback meal for lunch. She loves to pan fry thick slices of Spam, coating them in a sweet soy sauce mixture. Instead of giving out cookies, Mei has been known to share Spam musubi.

We have a musubi mold to shape the rice, but you can also use a cleaned-out Spam can. A fusion of Japanese onigiri, this savory and sweet meat over rice is great for a viewing of Lilo & Stitch *or* Moana.

Slice canned meat evenly into 8 pieces about ¼-inch thick. If you don't have a musubi mold, wash out the Spam container and dry. Line the Spam tin with plastic wrap. In a small bowl, mix the soy sauce and sugar. In a large skillet or cast-iron pan over medium heat, fry the Spam, about 1–2 minutes on each side. Add soy sauce sugar mixture to pan and cook until thicker and the Spam is coated, about 1 minute.

Add 1½ tablespoons or so of rice to the lined Spam container or musubi mold. This will make the bottom layer of rice. Place a slice of cooked Spam on the first rice layer. Top the Spam with another 1½ tablespoons of rice. Using the bottom of a spoon, press rice down to compact.

Remove from musubi mold, or if using the Spam can, pull the rice and spam from the tin using the corners of the plastic wrap. Place on a clean work surface and wrap with ⅓ sheet of nori, making a seaweed-like belt. Dip fingers in water to seal the nori sides together. Repeat steps until you have 8 pieces of Spam musubi.

LILO & STITCH
also *Moana*

SERVES 6–8

4–6 pounds pork shoulder
blade or butt, cut in half

Kosher salt or Hawaiian sea salt

1 tablespoon liquid
mesquite smoke

Kalua Pulled Pork

Traditionally cooked in an imu pit, or traditional underground oven, this smoky shredded pork dish is a Hawaiian staple. If you're like most of us and do not have the backyard space to smoke a whole pig underground for hours, this slow cooker method is the next best way. After cooking for hours, your home will be filled with the savory aroma of smoked salty pork. Great for a viewing of Lilo & Stitch *or* Moana.

In a slow cooker, add the pork halves and pierce with a fork. Generously sprinkle with salt, one teaspoon per pound of pork. Pour liquid smoke over the pork. Cook on low for 8–10 hours, or on high for 4 hours, then 2 hours on low.

Remove pork and about 2 cups of liquid from the slow cooker. Shred the pork and place in a large bowl. Add back the reserved liquid and mix, about ½ cup at a time. Add enough liquid to the pork until it looks moist, but is not swimming in the juice. The full two cups might not be needed. Add salt to taste. Serve warm. This pairs well with the Hawaiian Mac Salad.

SERVES 4

4 boneless skinless chicken
breasts (about 3 pounds)

Kosher salt, divided

Freshly ground black pepper

Canola oil for cooking

1 cup all-purpose flour

½ teaspoon garlic powder

½ teaspoon onion powder

2 eggs, beaten

3 cups panko breadcrumbs

Edna's Crispy Chicken Cutlets

The secret to crunchy pan-fried chicken is something I like to call the triple dip. First, you coat protein pieces in a layer of flour. Next, you dip them in egg wash. Last, you dunk the meat into panko breadcrumbs. The flour locks in the moisture, the egg helps the panko crumbs stick to the meat, and the fried panko keeps the chicken crisp and crunchy. Letting the chicken rest in its seasoning is an important step.

These crispy cutlets are good while you watch Edna Turnblad in Hairspray, *or as a base for the* Bugsy Malone–*inspired Fat Sam's Grand Slam Chicken Parmesan. Also the schnitzel for Von Trapp Schnitzel with Noodles for* The Sound of Music.

Place chicken breasts one at a time into a large gallon ziptop bag and seal. With a meat tenderizer, the bottom of a glass, or a rolling pin, lightly pound on the chicken until flat and about ¼ inch thick. Remove from bag and generously season with salt and pepper. Repeat for all chicken pieces. Let rest for about 20 minutes to give the salt time to season the chicken.

Heat a large skillet or cast-iron pan on medium heat. Add about an inch and a half of oil to cover the pan. Arrange 3 shallow-rimmed dishes, such as pie or cake pans, on your work surface. Whisk together the flour, garlic powder, onion powder, and 1 teaspoon of salt in one pan. Add the beaten eggs to the second pan and add the panko crumbs to the third.

Working in batches, fry the chicken by first dredging both sides of a flattened chicken breast through the flour mixture, dipping it in the egg, and then breading it with the panko crumbs. Carefully place the coated chicken in the hot oil. Cook on each side for 2–3 minutes, then place on a wire cooling rack. Repeat for each chicken breast. Serve warm.

SERVES 4

Tomato Sauce

1 (28-ounce) can whole tomatoes

5 cloves garlic, peeled

¼ cup extra-virgin olive oil

2 tablespoons tomato paste

1 teaspoon kosher salt

½ cup chopped fresh basil

Chicken

1 batch Edna's Crispy
Chicken Cutlets
(see recipe on page 105)

1 (12-ounce) package shredded
mozzarella cheese

1 (8-ounce) package shredded
Parmesan cheese

Fat Sam's Grand Slam Chicken Parmesan

Bugsy Malone was a new-to-me musical during our time of pandemic watching. The child actors are so animated, and I especially like the clever involvement of food in this movie (see recipe for Banoffee Pie, page 139). Fat Sam's Grand Slam is a tribute to the New York City speakeasy where anybody can be anybody.

This chicken Parmesan, with a crispy panko crust and rich tomato sauce, will satisfy any Prohibition-era New York gangster, child-sized or not.

To make the tomato sauce, blend the can of whole tomatoes and the garlic in a blender. Heat a large skillet over medium heat and pour in the blended tomato/garlic mixture. Add the olive oil. Mix in the tomato paste, salt, and chopped basil. Turn heat down to medium-low and simmer for 15 minutes.

Place fried chicken cutlets on a baking sheet. Top with tomato sauce and shredded mozzarella and Parmesan cheese. Broil on high until cheese is melted. Serve alone or on a bed of spaghetti, linguini, or angel hair pasta.

SERVES 6

Brown Gravy

4 cups beef stock

2 tablespoons soy sauce

2 tablespoons ketchup

2 teaspoons Worcestershire sauce

1 teaspoon kosher salt

4 tablespoons cornstarch

Hamburger Patties

1½ pounds ground beef

½ cup grated onion

1 tablespoon Worcestershire sauce

1 tablespoon soy sauce

½ cup panko breadcrumbs

½ teaspoon garlic powder

1½ teaspoons kosher salt

Canola oil for cooking

6 eggs

Cooked white rice

Furikake (optional)

2 green onions, chopped

Boat Snack Loco Moco

The fusion of food in Hawaii speaks to the blending of the many cultures on those numerous small islands. Invented in 1949 and named by Hawaiian teenagers, Loco Moco takes a Japanese version of hambagu, a beef patty served with ketchup-based sauce, and makes it island style.

With a large portion of rice, seasoned hamburger patty, and brown gravy, this mountain of food represents the generous spirit of the Aloha State. Top it with a fried egg sprinkled with furikake, a Japanese rice seasoning made up of nori seaweed, sesame seeds, and dried fish flakes, and you have a meal fit for any Hawaiian movie viewing.

In a large pot, whisk together the beef stock, soy sauce, ketchup, Worcestershire sauce, salt, and cornstarch. Cook over medium heat until thick and bubbly, about 5–8 minutes, whisking occasionally. Turn the heat to low to keep warm.

With your hands or a wooden spoon, mix together the ground beef, grated onion, Worcestershire sauce, soy sauce, breadcrumbs, garlic powder, and salt. Divide and form into six patties. On medium heat, coat a cast-iron pan or large nonstick skillet with oil. Cook 2–3 patties at a time in the hot pan, 3–4 minutes per side. Remove the hamburger patties and set aside.

In the same pan, wipe out the excess oil and/or crumbs and fry the eggs sunny-side up or over easy.

On a plate or bowl, scoop cooked, steamed rice. If using, sprinkle furikake over the rice. Place a hamburger patty and fried egg on top and pour brown gravy over the dish. Sprinkle chopped green onions. Repeat for each patty and serve immediately.

MAKES 40–45
MEATBALLS,
about 8–10
servings

1 pound ground beef

1 pound ground pork

½ cup panko breadcrumbs

½ cup grated onion

¼ cup fresh flat-leaf
parsley, chopped

2 garlic cloves, minced

1 teaspoon dried oregano

1 teaspoon ground coriander

1 teaspoon ground cumin

2 teaspoons kosher salt

½ teaspoon freshly
ground black pepper

1 egg, beaten

1 cup all-purpose flour, for coating

Canola oil for cooking

Hermes's Greek Meatballs

Keftedes, or traditional meatballs from Greece, are usually made with a combination of ground pork and beef. Infused with spices and chopped herbs, they are flavorful and tender.

I like to roll the meatballs in a little flour before cooking. When pan fried, this layer of flour helps give each meatball a crispy sear. These Greek meatballs work well as an entree, or as a gyro variation stuffed in a pita pocket with diced tomatoes and drizzled with The Muses' Cucumber Yogurt Tzatziki, or added to a salad with crumbled feta and a Greek vinaigrette.

In a large bowl, mix the beef, pork, panko breadcrumbs, onion, chopped parsley, minced garlic, dried oregano, coriander, cumin, salt, and black pepper. Stir in the beaten egg.

Divide the ground meat mixture to make 40 or so meatballs, each about the size of a whole walnut shell. Refrigerate for at least 1 hour. Place flour in a shallow rimmed dish, such as a pie plate. Lightly roll each meatball in the flour, coating all sides. Coat a large skillet or cast-iron pan with just enough oil to cover the pan, and place over medium heat.

Working in batches, cook the meatballs about 6–8 minutes each, rolling on to each side until browned. Serve warm.

SERVES 4–6

3 pounds dark-meat chicken
(about 8 thighs or 16 legs)

Kosher salt

Freshly ground black pepper

⅓ cup honey

3 tablespoons brown sugar

¼ cup soy sauce

2 tablespoons ginger, grated

2 cloves garlic, minced or grated

3 green onions, sliced

Cooked white rice (optional)

Jade Rabbit's Honey Soy Glazed Chicken

Sweet, savory, and simple, this honey soy glazed chicken is on regular rotation in the Bybee home. Thrown together and baked in a pan, the chicken is soaked in a soy marinade that also doubles as sauce. A one pan dish, this is an easy meal to get on the table on a busy night. This main course can be served alongside a salad or on top of hot white rice. A good choice for Over the Moon, Turning Red, *or* Mulan.

Preheat oven 425 degrees F. Line a 9x13 baking pan with aluminum foil. Add in the chicken, seasoning all sides with salt and pepper. In a large bowl, whisk the honey, brown sugar, soy sauce, ginger, and garlic. Pour this sauce over the chicken.

Bake the chicken, basting or spooning the soy sauce mixture from the pan over the meat every 10 minutes. Cook for 30–40 minutes or until meat is no longer pink. To add more color or crispiness, an optional step is to broil the chicken right after baking. Adjust the oven rack to the top two spots, placing the chicken close to the overhead heat. Set the broil heat to high and cook for a minute or less, just until the chicken starts to brown. Keep a close eye on the meat so it doesn't burn. Using a metal pan may be best; a glass dish may overheat under the broiler.

Top with green onions and serve immediately. The sauce in the pan can be used over the chicken or over a scoop of rice.

GREASE

MAKES 4
DOUBLE-PATTY
TURKEY BURGERS

Turkey Burger Patties

2 pounds 80/20 ground turkey

2 teaspoons kosher salt

Freshly ground black pepper

1 teaspoon garlic powder

2 eggs

2 tablespoons
Worcestershire sauce

½ cup onion, grated

½ cup panko breadcrumbs

Oil for cooking

Hamburger buns

Toppings

Mayonnaise

Yellow mustard

Sliced cheddar cheese

Tomato slices

Romaine or iceberg lettuce

Dill pickle slices

Polar Turkey Burgers

During the scene at the Frosty Diner in Grease, *the kids at Rydell High order a Double Polar Burger. Two beef patties make one big burger. Teenagers in the 1950s ate as much as the kids these days! This recipe is a favorite of Cassius, who loves a good hamburger (or two).*

In this rendition, I use ground turkey. The grated onion keeps the meat juicy, and the Worcestershire brings out the savory seasoning.

Sandwiched between soft hamburger buns, these patties are double-stacked quarter pounders with cheese. A popular item for any ne'er-do-well high-schooler, the jocks or the geeks.

In a large bowl, mix the ground turkey, salt, pepper, garlic powder, eggs, Worcestershire sauce, onion, and panko breadcrumbs together. Form quarter-pound (or about ½ cup) patties from the ground turkey mixture. Because the meat will shrink from cooking, make the patties about an inch wider in diameter than a regular hamburger bun.

Heat a large skillet or cast-iron pan on medium-high and coat with oil. Once hot, add the patties and fry for 2–3 minutes on each side. Be mindful to not move the patties while cooking. You'll want them to stay in contact with the hot pan as long as possible to get a brown and crusty surface.

Spread mayonnaise and mustard on the top and bottoms of a hamburger bun. Place one patty on the hamburger bun bottom and top with cheddar cheese. Add a slice of tomato and lettuce. Place the second turkey patty on the lettuce. Add another slice of cheese, tomato, pickles, and lettuce. Put the hamburger bun top on, and repeat all steps three more times.

SERVES 6

1 batch of Edna's Crispy
Chicken Cutlets
(see recipe on page 105)

1 pound egg noodles

¼ cup (½ stick) unsalted butter

Kosher salt

½ cup chopped fresh parsley

Lemon wedges

Von Trapp Schnitzel with Noodles

In my children's early years, noodles and butter were definitely a few of their favorite (and sometimes only) things they would eat. Who could blame them? Soft, but firm to the bite, any kind of pasta coated in a salty butter sauce is nothing to feel sad about. To Mei, who went through a picky eating toddler stage, it was about as cozy and comforting as a pair of warm woolen mittens.

Take a childhood favorite dish and add a side of schnitzel, or flat breaded cutlets, to elevate these noodles to a grown-up level.

Schnitzel is an Austrian specialty and a good recipe for The Sound of Music. *Served alongside plain buttered noodles, it fills the heart for the young and old alike.*

Boil the noodles in salted water according to package directions. Drain and place in a large bowl. Add butter, salt, and chopped parsley to the noodles, mix well, and serve with the lemon wedges and Edna's Crispy Chicken Schnitzel.

SONG OF THE SEA
also *The Little Mermaid*

SERVES 6

6 fillets of mild whitefish
(tilapia, cod, halibut)

1–1½ cups milk

Kosher salt, divided

Freshly ground black pepper

Canola oil for frying

1 cup all-purpose flour

½ teaspoon garlic powder

½ teaspoon onion powder

2 eggs, beaten

3 cups panko breadcrumbs

Selkie's Secret Pan-Fried Fish

While I'm not someone who minds the taste of the sea in fish, this recipe is for those of you who do. Soaking the fish in milk is my Selkie song secret. Like the mysterious shape shifting creatures that shed their seal skin to become human, milk also transforms a fishy fillet into something more neutral as it draws out odors or briny taste. Tilapia, with its lightly sweet and mild taste may help win over those with a hesitancy towards seafood.

Coated with a layer of seasoned panko breadcrumbs, this fish fries up crispy on the outside and remains flaky and tender on the inside. It may help those with an aversion to fish sing a new song.

Add fish fillets to a large bowl. Pour in just enough milk to cover the fish. Soak for 20 minutes. Remove, pat dry, and season the fish with salt and pepper to taste.

Heat a large skillet or cast-iron pan on medium heat. Add enough oil to generously cover the pan. Arrange 3 shallow-rimmed dishes, such as pie or cake pans, on your work surface. Whisk together the flour, garlic powder, onion powder, and 1 teaspoon of salt in one pan. Add the beaten eggs to the second pan and add the panko crumbs to the third.

Working in batches, fry the fish by first dredging a fillet through the flour mixture, coating it in the egg, breading it with the panko crumbs, and carefully placing it in the hot oil. Cook on each side for about 2 minutes until crust is golden brown. The fish should feel firm, and the fillet will be white and not translucent. Serve immediately.

MARY POPPINS
also *My Fair Lady*

SERVES 4–6

3 cups Bob Cratchit's Smooth Mashed Potatoes (see recipe on page 39)

½ cup all-purpose flour

1 egg

1 teaspoon kosher salt

½ cup (1 stick) unsalted butter, divided

1 cup onion, finely chopped

6 cups leftover cooked vegetables (such as cabbage, kale, Brussels sprouts, and carrots), chopped

Freshly ground black pepper

4–6 eggs, fried (optional)

Uncle Albert Bubble and Squeak Patties

Essentially a pan of fried leftover vegetables cooked in a batter of mashed potatoes, this pancake-like dish supposedly gets its quirky English name from the sound made while cooking. The veggies bubble up and "squeak" as they sizzle down in the pan. A similar dish in Ireland (just potatoes and cabbage) is called colcannon, and in Scotland, a related recipe (with both cabbage and turnips) is called rumbledethumps. Can these names get any better? Served as a hearty break-fast or for brunch, these scrummy patties will help any cook feel completely chuffed in the kitchen.

In a large bowl, mix together the mashed potatoes, flour, egg, and salt. Set aside.

In a large skillet or cast-iron pan, melt ¼ cup butter over medium heat. Add chopped onions and sauté until soft and brown on the edges, about 5–7 minutes.

Add the chopped vegetables. Pan fry for 4–6 minutes or until veggies cook down. Add the cooked vegetables to the mashed potato mixture. Form into balls and press into patties. Add the remaining ¼ cup butter to the pan. Fry the potato patties for about 3–5 minutes or until the potato starts to brown. As the potato and vegetables cook, the patties will start to make a faint squeaking sound as they dry out from the heat. Flip over and fry on the other side. Cook for another 3–5 minutes or until the potato starts to brown. Top with optional fried or poached egg and serve alongside sausages or a green salad.

FROZEN
also *White Christmas*

SERVES 1

3 slices of bread, toasted
(white or potato preferred)

¼ cup mayonnaise

2 romaine or iceberg lettuce leaves

½ large tomato, sliced

Salt and pepper, to taste

2 ounces sliced turkey

1 slice cheddar cheese

2 ounces sliced ham

3 slices cooked bacon

We Finish Each Other's Turkey, Ham, and Bacon Club Sandwiches

Stacked high with meat, cheese, vegetables, and a third slice of bread, these club sandwiches aren't your ordinary lunchtime fare. In our house, Selah loves sandwiches. Her favorite combo includes everything in this double-decker club, with the addition of a dill pickle on the side. When she was younger, her favorite musical was Frozen, *where there is a great line about finishing each other's sandwiches.*

These sandwiches are huge. While the serving size says one, it can easily be shared. And a big shout-out to club sandwiches in White Christmas, *where they were served on the train in a club car. As the four main leads make plans to go to the Columbia Inn in Pine Tree, Vermont, sparks fly. There was great chemistry between the couples from this scene on. Maybe it was the winter wonderland idea of Vermont, the plan to save the failing inn—or maybe . . . it was the sandwiches.*

On a clean working surface such as a large cutting board, lay out three slices of toast. Spread mayonnaise on one side of each slice. Place 2 lettuce leaves on the first slice of bread, then top with tomato slices and season with salt and pepper. Add 2 ounces of sliced turkey. Add the second piece of toast and top with a slice of cheese, 2 ounces of sliced ham, and 3 slices of bacon.

Top sandwich with the third piece of toast, mayonnaise side down. Press down slightly to compact everything together. With a serrated knife, cut the sandwich diagonally into two halves. If needed, pierce a toothpick into the center of each slice to keep secure. Serve immediately.

FINALE

Like the closing act of a musical, this finale is the chance to captivate your audience and bring it home big. These home-made desserts will leave a lasting impression on an already spectacular meal and may have the crowd shouting, "Encore!"

Desserts

The Babe's Brown Butter Rice Cereal Treats
Labyrinth 127

Baked Alaska Ice Cream Cake
Annie 128

Violet's Blueberry Hand Pies
Willy Wonka and the Chocolate Factory 131

One More Slice Chocolate Cake
Matilda 132

Caramel Bacon Hello Dollies
Hello Dolly! 135

Chocolate River Torte
Willy Wonka and the Chocolate Factory 136

Dandy Dan's Banoffee Pie
Bugsy Malone 139

Cast Iron Skillet Chocolate Chip Cookie
Tangled 140

High Tide Coconut Butter Mochi
Moana 143

Gray Stuff Crushed Cookie Frosting
Beauty and the Beast 144

That Guy We Don't Talk About's
Triple Milk Rice Pudding
Encanto 147

Headmistress Homemade
Chocolate Hobnobs
Matilda 148

Mount Olympus Orange Honey
Baklava Bars
Hercules 151

Shortbread Finger Cookies
Hocus Pocus 152

Very Vanilla Unbirthday Cupcakes
Alice in Wonderland 155

Toppings

Sideshow Strawberry Frosting
The Greatest Showman 156

Barnum's Salted
Caramel Sauce
The Greatest Showman . . 159

Showstopper
Hot Fudge Sauce
The Greatest Showman 159

Big Top Whipped Cream
The Greatest Showman 160

SERVES 20

Nonstick baking spray
or parchment paper

1 cup (2 sticks) unsalted butter

1 (16-ounce) bag mini
marshmallows

½ teaspoon kosher salt

1 teaspoon vanilla extract

1 (12-ounce) box toasted rice
cereal, such as Rice Krispies

1 (10-ounce) bag mini
marshmallows

Flaked sea salt

The Babe's Brown Butter Rice Cereal Treats

Invented in 1920 by Iowa's Mildred Day, Rice Krispies treats are an American dessert staple. There are perhaps hundreds of adaptations of this cereal-and-marshmallow delight. Over the years, I may have tinkered with them all.

I've found that my preference for Rice Krispies treats is this: I like them soft, with lots and lots of gooey marshmallow. Also—tall, so thick you can hardly put your mouth around the first bite. This variation leans a bit extra on the marshmallows: one large bag of mini marshmallows melted to hold the cereal together and another bag for additional fluff and goodness. Brown butter makes them rich and decadent, an updated take on a classic treat. I think Mildred would be pleased to know how far her influence has come.

Spray a 9x13 baking pan with nonstick baking spray or line with parchment paper. Set aside.

In a large soup pot or Dutch oven, melt the butter over medium heat. Using a heatproof spatula or wooden spoon, stir or swirl the pan constantly for about 5–7 minutes until the butter is golden or light tan in color. As it browns, the butter will start to bubble and foam.

With the butter browned, add in the larger bag of marshmallows. Continue to gently stir as the marshmallows start to melt. Add the kosher salt. With the first bag of marshmallows completely melted, turn off the heat and stir in the vanilla extract.

Starting with the cereal, alternate cereal and half the bag of 10-ounce mini marshmallows until all stirred in. Note: these marshmallows will not melt completely but will give extra pockets of gooey goodness.

Scoop the mixture into the prepared 9x13 pan. It will take up the entire pan, with excess on top. Gently pat down into the pan, being careful not to press too hard. Sprinkle flaked sea salt on top and let cool for at least 30 minutes. Flip the pan over onto a cutting board to release the rice cereal. Cut the treats into large squares and serve.

ANNIE
also *High School Musical*

SERVES 10–12

½ gallon ice cream, slightly softened

One More Slice Chocolate Cake (see recipe on page 132)

Italian Meringue

½ cup water

1 cup granulated sugar

Whites of 4 eggs, room temperature

½ teaspoon cream of tartar

Butane kitchen torch

Baked Alaska Ice Cream Cake

Inspired by the 1867 Russian land deal that eventually added Alaska as the 49th state, this meringue-topped dessert was the original ice cream cake. I didn't hear about it until the 1980s, when I was a young kid watching Annie. *On the first day at Daddy Warbucks's mansion, the cook announces that Baked Alaska was on the menu.*

Essentially an ice cream cake coated with swirly meringue, this treat needs a modern-day comeback. Thick ribbons of marshmallow meringue serve as insulation for the frozen treat. Make the chocolate cake ahead of time, and this recipe can be a fun dessert to assemble together.

Line a 9-inch, 2.5-quart bowl with plastic wrap, using enough extra plastic to hang over sides for easy removal. Fill the lined bowl with softened ice cream to create a dome shape. Cover the top of the ice cream with additional plastic wrap and place in the freezer for at least eight hours or overnight.

Once the ice cream is frozen hard, remove the bowl from the freezer. Remove the top layer of plastic wrap and place the cooled chocolate cake on top of the ice cream. Put the cake and ice cream back in the freezer and freeze them together for at least another 30 minutes.

While the ice cream cake hardens, make the meringue. In a stainless steel saucepan over medium heat, add the water and granulated sugar. Stir together just once. Allow the mixture to come to a boil, about 3–5 minutes. The sugar water syrup should be clear, with all sugar crystals dissolved. The mixture will be bubbly. Continue to cook for another 3–5 minutes, until a digital thermometer reads 230 degrees F. Turn heat off and remove pan from heat.

In the bowl of a stand mixer fitted with the whisk attachment, whip the egg whites at medium-high. After a few minutes, the mixture will be foamy. Pour the sugar syrup into the egg whites in a steady stream, aiming for the side of the bowl, and continue to mix on high speed, and as peaks start to form, add the cream of tartar. Continue to whip until stiff peaks form, about five minutes.

Take the ice cream/cake out of the freezer. Invert onto a heat-proof serving platter (cake side down) and carefully remove bowl and plastic wrap. Working quickly, top the ice cream dome with the meringue, completely covering the entire surface, making swoopy peaks and swirls in the meringue with the back of a large spoon.

Carefully use a butane kitchen torch to toast the meringue (this is a job for an adult). If you do not have a kitchen torch, place the cake in the oven under the broiler on high until the topping is just browned. With a sharp or serrated knife, cut into slices and serve immediately. Place leftovers in freezer.

MAKES 6 HAND PIES

1 (17.3-ounce) package
puff pastry, thawed

Blueberry Filling

2½ cups fresh or frozen blueberries

⅓ cup granulated sugar

¼ teaspoon kosher salt

1 tablespoon fresh lemon juice

2 tablespoons cornstarch

Egg Wash

1 egg, beaten

Blueberry Glaze

1½ cups confectioners' sugar

2 tablespoons blueberry filling

1–2 tablespoons milk

Violet's Blueberry Hand Pies

With a blueberry glaze almost violet in color, these hand pies are a purple sight to behold. Nestled in between premade puff pastry dough are spoonfuls of sweet and tart blueberry filling. The cutout circles bake up flaky in the oven and are a fun project for kids to "paint" the glaze on. Serve these individual pies for a viewing of Willy Wonka and the Chocolate Factory *or alongside other pastries for an* Alice in Wonderland *tea party.*

Heat oven to 425 degrees F. and place rack in the center. Line a baking sheet with parchment paper and set aside.

Roll out the puff pastry dough and cut out 12 (4-inch diameter) circles. These will make 6 hand pies. Place in refrigerator until use.

In a medium-sized saucepan over medium heat, add the fresh or frozen blueberries, sugar, salt, lemon juice, and cornstarch. Cook until berries break down and liquid thickens, about 5 minutes. Remove from heat. Reserve 2–3 tablespoons of filling for the blueberry glaze.

Take puff pastry circles out of the refrigerator. On a clean work surface, lay out 6 pastry circles. Place 2 tablespoons of filling in the middle of one circle. Brush the perimeter of the circle with egg wash. Place another pastry circle on top and seal the edges. Repeat for the remaining 5 circles. Cut slits into the top of the pies. Brush each pie with the remaining egg wash and bake for 20–22 minutes, or until tops are golden brown. Remove from oven and allow to cool.

In a small bowl, make the glaze by whisking together the confectioners' sugar and ½ teaspoon of reserved blueberry filling. Add milk 1 tablespoon at a time or more as needed to thin. Paint the purple glaze on each hand pie and serve.

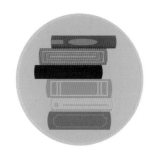

MAKES 2 (9-INCH)
ROUND LAYER CAKES,
or 1 (9x13) sheet cake,
or 24 cupcakes

Nonstick baking spray
2 cups all-purpose flour, plus
more for flouring pans
2 cups granulated sugar
¾ cup cocoa powder
2 teaspoons baking soda
1 teaspoon baking powder
1 teaspoon kosher salt
1 cup sour cream
½ cup (1 stick) unsalted butter,
room temperature
½ cup vegetable oil
2 eggs, room temperature
2 teaspoons vanilla extract
1 tablespoon roasted barley
beverage mix, such as Pero
1 cup hot water

Cocoa Chocolate Frosting
Makes about 5 cups

1 cup (2 sticks) salted butter
6 cups confectioners' sugar
¾ cup cocoa powder
2 teaspoons vanilla extract
4-6 tablespoons heavy cream

One More Slice Chocolate Cake

Like me, Selah loves a good bake. One day, she inadvertently added a stick of butter reserved for the frosting into my recipe for chocolate cake. It was a happy accident! This extra ingredient makes the cake ultra-rich, with a really great crumb. I like to use Pero, a coffee-free substitute made from malted barley, chicory, and rye. This natural powder gives the chocolate an extra boost and can be found in the coffee and tea aisle.

One of the best scenes involving chocolate cake in a musical happens in Matilda. *Don't we all want to be like Bruce, who takes on the chocolate cake challenge? Grab a huge spoon, a hanky for under your chin, and cheer for anyone who can polish off this entire cake by themselves.*

Preheat oven to 350 degrees F. Using baking spray or butter, grease and flour two 9-inch round cake pans or one 9x13 pan. For round cakes, place parchment paper circles on the bottom of each pan. If making cupcakes, line 2 cupcake pans with cupcake liners.

In a large bowl, whisk together the flour, sugar, cocoa powder, baking soda, baking powder, and salt. In the bowl of a stand mixer fitted with the paddle attachment, add sour cream, butter, vegetable oil, eggs, and vanilla. Mix on medium-low speed until combined. Add in the bowl of dry ingredients and mix together on low speed until just combined. In a medium bowl, stir the Pero into the hot water. Add this mixture into the cake batter and stir in on low speed.

Pour the batter into the prepared pans and bake for 35–40 minutes. To check if the cake is finished, insert a toothpick in the center of a cake. It's done when the toothpick comes out clean with a few crumbs attached. Remove from oven and allow to cool on a wire rack. Run a plastic butter knife along the circumference of the pan to help release the cake from the pan. Allow to cool to room temperature before frosting.

For Cocoa Chocolate Frosting

In the bowl of a stand mixer fitted with the paddle attachment, cream the butter on medium speed. Reduce speed to low and gradually add in confectioners' sugar one cup at a time. Scraping down the sides, add in cocoa powder. When all the sugar and cocoa are mixed in, add in the vanilla, then the cream one tablespoon at a time. Add in more cream to desired consistency. Mix for 2 minutes. Increase speed to medium-high or high and beat for an additional 3–4 minutes. The frosting should be light and fluffy.

HELLO DOLLY!

MAKES 24 BARS

Nonstick baking spray

1 recipe graham cracker crust (see Dandy Dan's Banoffee Pie recipe on page 139)

1 (13.4-ounce) can dulce de leche

1 (14-ounce) can sweetened condensed milk

2 cups shredded sweetened coconut

1½ cups semisweet chocolate chips

1 cup salted roasted pecans, or any combination of roasted nuts

½ cup cooked crispy bacon, chopped

Caramel Bacon Hello Dollies

Growing up, I did not know of the musical Hello Dolly! *or of the Hello Dolly bars dessert. However, I did know Barbara Streisand; she was one of my mom's favorite actors. Yet this musical had completely escaped me.*

When we watched Hello Dolly! *during our year-long project, I couldn't help but think how happy Mom would have been to know her grandkids were being introduced to this striking and amazing woman. The restaurant scene at Harmonia Gardens is the stuff of Broadway legends. This high-end eatery captured Dolly's heart, as did their stuffed chicken dinner.*

With crisp, salty bacon pieces folded in between mounds of sweet coconut and chocolate, I think this version of Hello Dollies will also become the stuff of dreams. A buttery crust of crushed graham crackers lays the foundation of these chocolate coconut bars. They are salty and sweet. Memorable and bold. Just like Dolly Levi herself.

Preheat oven to 350 degrees F. Line 9x13 baking pan with parchment paper and spray the pan with baking spray. Cover the bottom layer of the pan with the graham cracker crust, pressing it to about ¼-inch thickness.

In a medium bowl, whisk the dulce de leche and sweetened condensed milk together. Pour half of this mixture on top of the graham cracker crust. In another medium bowl, toss the coconut, chocolate chips, nuts, and bacon together. Sprinkle on top of the first dulce de leche layer. Drizzle the remaining dulce de leche/condensed milk mixture on top of the coconut, chocolate chips, nuts, and bacon.

Bake for 30–40 minutes or until golden brown on top. Allow to cool on wire rack until pan comes to room temperature, then refrigerate for an hour or until firm. Cut into bars and serve.

FINALE: Desserts and Toppings

MAKES ONE 8-INCH
OR 9-INCH CAKE

Nonstick baking spray

1⅓ cups chopped chocolate, like semisweet chocolate chips

1 cup (2 sticks) salted butter

1 cup granulated sugar

5 eggs, room temperature

½ teaspoon kosher salt

1 teaspoon vanilla extract

1 tablespoon cocoa powder

Optional Toppings

Confectioners' sugar

1 recipe Big Top Whipped Cream (see recipe on page 160)

Fresh fruit

Chocolate River Torte

Inspired by Molly Wizenberg's Winning Hearts and Mind Cake, this dessert has been in my repertoire for years. With no flour, these thick wedges of chocolate cake are fudgy and gluten-free. It's elegant, yet simple in complexity with just six ingredients—and one bowl! This dessert is even better the next day. If you can, give it time to chill in the fridge or even the freezer. With this overnight rest, the texture becomes smooth and the flourless cake fudgy.

To elevate this to special, use the best quality chocolate. However, even regular semisweet chocolate chips will make an indulgent treat. For a thicker cake, use an 8-inch cake pan. A generous slice topped with whipped cream or fresh fruit makes this a great dessert for Willy Wonka and the Chocolate Factory *or* My Fair Lady.

Preheat oven to 375 degrees F. With cooking spray, grease an 8-inch or 9-inch round cake pan. Line the bottom of the pan with a round circle of parchment paper. Spray this liner and flour the pan.

Place the chopped chocolate and the butter in a microwavable medium bowl. Microwave on high in 30-second intervals, stirring often, until just smooth.

Remove bowl from microwave and stir in the sugar. Next, whisk in the eggs one at a time. After all the eggs are mixed in, whisk in the salt, vanilla, and cocoa powder.

Pour cake batter into the pan. Bake for 30–40 minutes or until a toothpick inserted into the middle comes out with a few crumbs attached. Check frequently, the cake will look slightly underdone. This is good! Time in the refrigerator will help solidify the cake and gives it the fudge-like texture. Remove from oven, and allow the cake to cool on a wire rack for another 10 minutes. While resting, the cake will continue to cook.

Run a plastic butter knife along the edge of the pan to loosen. Place in refrigerator or freezer for two hours or until firm. Once cooled and solid, release cake onto a cutting board and peel off parchment paper. Cut into wedges and serve topped with a sprinkling of confectioners' sugar, whipped cream, or fruit.

BUGSY MALONE
also *Mary Poppins*

Graham Cracker Pie Crust

MAKES ONE 9-INCH
PIE CRUST

1 sleeve (9 sheets) graham crackers

½ teaspoon kosher salt

3 tablespoons granulated sugar

⅓ cup unsalted butter, melted

Banoffee Pie

MAKES ONE 9-INCH PIE

1 prepared graham cracker
crust (see recipe above)

1 (13.4-ounce) can dulce de leche

2 large bananas, peeled and sliced

1 recipe Big Top Whipped Cream
(see recipe on page 160)

Chocolate sprinkles or shavings

Dandy Dan's Banoffee Pie

Created in England in 1971 (the same year Bugsy Malone *was released), Banoffee Pie is a British take on an American compilation of banana cream and toffee. Layers of banana slices, thick dulce de leche, and fluffy whipped cream come together in this ultra-rich, extremely intense dessert. I think the hodgepodge name of Banoffee is fitting for* Bugsy Malone. *With musical roots and shared productions in the United States and the United Kingdom, like the pie, it also straddles two continents.*

In this New York City gangster film, adult roles are played by pint-sized child actors. They are quite adorable, yet also fierce. Being a movie about the Mob, expect some action, but make it fun. For ammunition, whipped cream is used for bullets. Cream pies are used to take people out. Let's just say there is a lot of whipped cream used in this movie.

To make this pie, the only use of the oven is in assembling the graham cracker crust. Next come the bananas and dulce de leche for toffee. Finished with a fluffy white mountain of whipped cream, this can also be a good British pick for a viewing of Mary Poppins.

For Graham Cracker Pie Crust

Preheat oven to 350 degrees F. and set the rack to the middle.

Place the graham crackers, salt, and sugar in a gallon-size ziptop bag. Use a rolling pin to grind crackers into coarse crumbs. Add the sugared cracker crumbs and the melted butter into a 9-inch pie pan. Toss with your fingers to combine. Press the crust into the pan, working on the outer rim first, then the center. Bake the crust for 8–10 minutes, until edges are slightly brown. Allow to cool.

For Banoffee Pie

Once the graham cracker crust has cooled, fill with dulce de leche and spread evenly throughout the pan. Layer sliced bananas on top. Top with whipped cream and sprinkle chocolate sprinkles or chocolate shavings on top.

FINALE: Desserts and Toppings

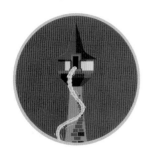

1 cup all-purpose flour

½ teaspoon baking soda

1 teaspoon kosher salt

½ cup (1 stick) unsalted butter

½ cup brown sugar

⅓ cup granulated sugar

1 egg

1 egg yolk

1 teaspoon vanilla extract

1 cup semisweet chocolate chips

Cast Iron Skillet Chocolate Chip Cookie

I would like to see cast iron skillets make more wedding and kitchen essentials registries. Why aren't these hefty, heavy-bottom pans at the top of everyone's wish list? They are practically nonstick, distribute heat evenly, and maintain a consistent cooking temperature. Sure, they're a little clunky. Cleanup can take some getting used to (no metal scouring pads, ever). However, the versatility of this pan is worth the effort and patience.

In Tangled, Rapunzel knew that the common cast-iron skillet is a formidable weapon. Another use wonderful use for this pan? Dessert.

Essentially a large cookie baked in a pan, this Cast Iron Skillet Chocolate Chip Cookie recipe is a keeper. Cooking in the cast iron gives this cookie a crispy outer crust with a chewy center.

Buttering the pan isn't to prevent the batter from sticking, but to help give it golden edges and a crisp exterior. If you like this cookie a little gooier, bake for a shorter amount of time. Serve cut into pie-shaped triangles or with a scoop of ice cream on top.

Preheat the oven to 350 degrees F. Grease a 10-inch cast-iron skillet with butter and set aside. In a medium bowl, whisk together the flour, baking soda, and salt.

Using a standing mixer or an electric mixer, beat the unsalted butter, brown sugar, and granulated sugar on medium speed for about three minutes. Add the egg, egg yolk, and vanilla. Add the whisked dry ingredients to the bowl and slowly mix until all is incorporated. Add in the chocolate chips.

Spread the batter evenly into the cast-iron skillet. Bake for 25–30 minutes or until the top of the cookie is golden brown. For a gooier cookie, bake for 20–25 minutes. For a gooey center, serve this treat immediately. To have a firmer cookie, allow to cool in the skillet for an additional 15–30 minutes. The cookie will continue to cook in the pan. Cut into wedges and serve.

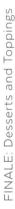

MOANA
also *Lilo & Stitch*

MAKES 24 SQUARES

1 (16-ounce) package (or 3 cups) mochiko rice flour

2 teaspoons baking powder

½ teaspoon salt

4 large eggs

½ cup (1 stick) unsalted butter, melted

2 cups granulated sugar

2 (14-ounce) cans unsweetened coconut milk

1 teaspoon vanilla extract

½ cup dried sweetened shredded coconut

High Tide Coconut Butter Mochi

If you aren't familiar with mochiko, or sweet rice flour, don't be alarmed. Mochiko flour gives this cake a bouncy texture and unique chew while the shredded coconut topping gives texture and added depth. The mochiko rice flour is a specialty item and may not be found in your neighborhood market. No worry, beef curry. Order online, or go shopping at an Asian grocery store. Most mochiko flour comes in 16-ounce packages, and one box makes one batch.

This recipe is baked in a 9x13 pan and cut into squares. They resemble brownies in shape and size, looking more like their blond surfer cousins.

For a family night viewing of Moana *or* Lilo & Stitch, *this dessert will transport you to a land of palm trees and white sandy beaches.*

Preheat oven to 350 degrees F. and place rack in the center. Grease a 9x13 baking pan and line the bottom with parchment paper.

In a medium bowl, whisk together rice flour, baking powder, and salt. Set aside dry ingredients. In a large bowl, whisk the eggs. Add melted butter, sugar, coconut milk, and vanilla. Continue to stir for two to four minutes until pale yellow. Add the dry ingredients and mix until incorporated. Pour batter into the prepared 9x13 baking pan and top carefully with sweetened shredded coconut. Bake for 50-60 minutes. The cake and shredded coconut should be light golden brown. Place pan on wire rack and allow to cool completely. Cut into squares and serve. Can be kept in an airtight container at room temperature for up to three days.

MAKES ABOUT 5 CUPS,
enough to frost a
2-layer 9-inch cake
or 24 cupcakes

1 cup (2 sticks) salted butter

6 cups confectioners' sugar

½ cup (about 6–8 cookies)
crushed chocolate sandwich
cookies, such as Oreo

1 teaspoon vanilla extract

4–6 tablespoons heavy cream

Gray Stuff Crushed Cookie Frosting

Try this gray stuff, it's delicious! Made from crushed cookies, this frosting is not at all French, but a fun recipe inspired by Beauty and the Beast. *Pipe on mini cupcakes for a playfully sweet hors d'oeuvre.*

In the bowl of a stand mixer fitted with the paddle attachment, cream butter on medium speed. Reduce speed to low and gradually add in confectioners' sugar, 1 cup at a time. Scraping down the sides, add in the crushed chocolate cookies. When all the sugar and crushed cookies are mixed in, add in the vanilla and cream, 1 tablespoon at a time. Mix for 2 minutes. Increase speed to medium-high or high and beat for an additional 3–4 minutes. The frosting should be light and fluffy.

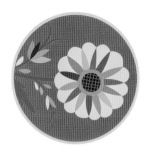

1 cup Arborio, or another long-grain rice, such as jasmine

1 (14-ounce) can sweetened condensed milk

1 (14-ounce) can unsweetened coconut milk

4 cups milk

½ teaspoon ground cinnamon

¼ teaspoon ground nutmeg

2 teaspoons vanilla extract

Topping

Big Top Whipped Cream, optional (see recipe on page 160)

That Guy We Don't Talk About's Triple Milk Rice Pudding

This creamy smooth rice pudding is a spin on a tres leches cake, a Latin American dessert that means "three-milk" cake. It's filling, warm, and sweet. I lean towards one pot types of recipes and appreciate how the rice cooks in the milk. No separate rice instructions here.

I also like the rice to cook down super soft and fine. As this starch breaks down, it helps thicken the pudding. This version cooks longer than traditional arroz con tres leches (three-milk rice). If you prefer your rice to have more bite, take it off the heat sooner. Finish with an optional heaping of whipped cream. That Guy We Don't Talk About's Triple Milk Rice Pudding can be served for a celebration of Encanto *or* Coco.

In a large stockpot on medium heat, add rice, sweetened condensed milk, coconut milk, and milk. Stir in the cinnamon and nutmeg. Bring to a boil, then lower the heat to medium-low. Stir occasionally to prevent the rice from sticking to the bottom of the pot and cook for about 45 minutes to an hour. As the rice breaks down, it will absorb the milk and the pudding will thicken. Remove from heat and stir in the vanilla. If the pudding is too solid, add more milk to thin. Serve warm.

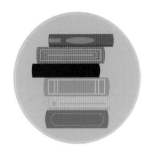

MAKES 4 DOZEN

2 cups old-fashioned oats

1½ cups all-purpose flour

¾ teaspoon baking powder

½ teaspoon baking soda

1½ teaspoons kosher salt

1 cup (2 sticks) unsalted butter

1 cup granulated sugar

¼ cup light brown sugar

1 egg

1 cup semisweet chocolate
chips for melting

Headmistress Homemade Chocolate Hobnobs

With crunchy, crumbly oats and the quirkiest of names, Hobnobs are quintessentially British. The cookie is buttery and crisp, baked thin, and brown-sugar sweet. A coating of semisweet chocolate may be optional, but not if I were the headmistress of the school (or household). Served alongside hot cocoa for dunking, this is a good biscuit for snacking on while watching Matilda *or* Song of the Sea.

Preheat oven to 350 degrees F. Line a half-sheet baking pan with parchment paper.

In a large bowl, whisk together the oats, flour, baking powder, baking soda, and salt. In the bowl of a stand mixer fitted with the paddle attachment, cream the butter on medium speed. Add the white and brown sugars and continue to mix until butter and sugar are light and fluffy, about 2–3 minutes. Stir in the egg and continue to mix. Add in the dry ingredients, mixing until just incorporated. Stir with a silicone spatula, scraping down the sides.

Roll out small balls (about 1½ inches in diameter) of cookie dough. Place on the prepared half-sheet baking pan about 3 inches apart. With the bottom of a glass or jar, flatten the balls of dough into ¼-inch thick rounds. Bake for 12–15 minutes or until golden brown. Allow to rest on the pan for a couple of minutes, then remove and allow to cool on a wire rack.

In a small glass bowl melt semisweet chocolate chips in 30-second intervals in the microwave. Spread chocolate on top of each cookie and allow to cool.

MAKES 2 DOZEN

Sugar Cookie Bar

Nonstick baking spray

2½ cups all-purpose flour

1 cup (2 sticks) unsalted butter, room temperature

½ teaspoon kosher salt

1 (8-ounce) package cream cheese, room temperature

1 cup granulated sugar

½ cup confectioners' sugar

1 large egg, room temperature

1 teaspoon vanilla extract

Baklava Topping

1½ cups chopped walnuts (or a mix of nuts)

½ cup granulated sugar

¼ cup unsalted butter, softened

1 teaspoon ground cinnamon

¼ teaspoon kosher salt

Frozen phyllo dough shells (from 2.1-ounce package)

Orange-Honey Glaze

¼ cup honey

2 tablespoons unsalted butter

1 tablespoon brown sugar

1 tablespoon orange juice

¼ teaspoon cinnamon

¼ teaspoon kosher salt

1 teaspoon vanilla extract

Mount Olympus Orange Honey Baklava Bars

The combination of thin pastry dough, finely chopped nuts, and syrupy honey is something that would surely please the Greek gods. You can go the distance and make this flaky layered dessert the traditional way by soaking each layer with honey and lemon.

Or, try this twist on baklava as a reimagined bar cookie. Soft sugar cookie dough is topped with chopped nuts, crumbled phyllo sheets, and baked together. A little drizzle of orange syrup and this dessert transforms into something us mere mortals can make.

Preheat oven to 350 degrees F. Lightly spray a 9x13 baking pan with nonstick baking spray. Line the pan with parchment paper.

In a medium bowl, whisk together the flour and salt. In the bowl of a stand mixer fitted with the paddle attachment, beat butter and cream cheese on medium speed until well blended, about 1 minute. Mix in the granulated and confectioners' sugars. Beat until smooth, about 1 minute. Add the egg and vanilla and beat on low speed until well combined, about 1 minute. Turn off the mixer and scrape down the bowl with a rubber spatula. Gradually add in the flour mixture, mixing on low speed just until blended, about 1 minute.

Using a spatula, scrape the dough into the prepared baking pan. Using damp fingers or a greased offset spatula, spread the dough into an even layer. Bake for 15 minutes. The cookie bars will not be quite done. Remove from oven, but keep oven at 350 degrees F.

For Baklava Topping

In a medium bowl, stir together the walnuts, granulated sugar, butter, cinnamon, and salt. Mixture will be crumbly. Sprinkle the nut mixture evenly over partially baked sugar cookie bars. With your hands, crumble frozen phyllo evenly over the nut mixture. Bake 18 to 20 minutes longer or until golden brown. Remove from oven and allow to cool.

For Orange-Honey Glaze

In a small microwavable bowl, microwave honey, butter, brown sugar, orange juice, cinnamon, and salt. Remove from microwave and stir in vanilla. Drizzle honey mixture evenly over bars. Allow to cool completely, about 2 hours, before cutting into bars and serving.

HOCUS POCUS
also *The Nightmare Before Christmas*

MAKES APPROXIMATELY 36 COOKIES

1 cup (2 sticks) unsalted butter

1 egg yolk

1 cup confectioners' sugar

2 cups all-purpose flour

¾ teaspoon kosher salt

Cocoa powder and/or green food coloring (optional)

Various nuts, such as pine nuts, whole almonds, or sliced almonds

Shortbread Finger Cookies

Made from just a few ingredients, this simple shortbread is substantial as it is delicate. Buttery and soft, the dough is flexible for straightforward molding. For a spooky treat, round the pastry into finger-like short stubby cylinders. Placing a nut at the end of each cookie takes this treat to a terrible level. The sliced nuts are brittle and thin, resembling yellowed nails once baked. A horrifying but delicious treat for any Halloween musical, such as Hocus Pocus *or* The Nightmare Before Christmas.

Preheat the oven to 300 degrees F. Line a half-sheet baking pan with parchment paper and set aside.

In the bowl of a stand mixer fitted with the paddle attachment, cream butter on medium speed. Add in the egg yolk. Turn the speed to low and slowly add in the confectioners' sugar. Slowly mix in the flour and salt. Turn speed back to medium and mix until all the ingredients are incorporated, about 1 minute. Remove the cookie dough and press into a ball, gently kneading in the loose crumbs.

If you'd like the fingers to be different tones, divide the dough and mix in some cocoa powder or green food coloring—just enough to change the dough color.

To shape into fingers, take a ball of dough (no exact measurement here, it all depends on how large you want the cookies to be) and roll into a bumpy log. I try to leave as many cracks and imperfections as possible in these cookies. I think they add more character to the gnarled-looking finger. You can also cut in wrinkles with a butter knife. Place the finger in the prepared half-sheet baking pan. Place one nut on the tip of the finger cookie and press gently to make the "fingernail." If the nut cracks or is already chipped, no problem. These blemishes make the finger look even better. Repeat, leaving about an inch between each cookie. They will expand slightly in the oven. Bake for 18–20 minutes or until just golden brown. The cookies will lose some of their form when baking—you can re-form them while the dough is still warm to exaggerate their crooked features.

MAKES 12 CUPCAKES
or 48 mini cupcakes

2 cups cake flour

1½ teaspoons baking powder

1 teaspoon baking soda

½ teaspoon salt

½ cup (1 stick) unsalted
butter, room temperature

1 cup granulated sugar

2 eggs, room temperature

½ cup sour cream

¼ cup canola oil

1 tablespoon vanilla extract

⅔ cup whole milk

Very Vanilla Unbirthday Cupcakes

This classic vanilla cupcake recipe is a staple in our household. Used for everyday "unbirth-days" or actual milestones, it's a great cake to celebrate anything.

Lighter than all-purpose flour, cake flour helps these cupcakes stay soft and delicate. While light and airy, they aren't lightweights in flavor. These vanilla cupcakes bake up sturdy. Top with your choice of frosting (see, for example, the Cocoa Chocolate Frosting recipe on page 132, Gray Stuff Crushed Cookie Frosting recipe on page 144, or Sideshow Strawberry Frosting recipe on page 156) and decorate with sprinkles for a fun party dessert.

Preheat oven to 350 degrees F. and place rack in the center. Line 1 (12-cup) cupcake pan or 2 (24-cup) mini cupcake pans with liners.

In a medium bowl, whisk together the flour, baking powder, baking soda, and salt. In the bowl of a stand mixer fitted with the paddle attachment, beat the butter, adding in the sugar, and mix until light and creamy, about 3–5 minutes. Add in eggs one at a time and mix. While mixing slowly on medium-low, add in the sour cream, oil, vanilla, and milk. Add in the flour mixture on low speed. Mix until just combined.

Divide the batter into the cupcake pans, filling each cup ¾ full. Bake until a toothpick inserted into the middle of the cupcakes comes out clean, about 15–18 minutes for regular cupcakes, 8–10 minutes for mini cupcakes. Allow to cool on a wire rack for 10 minutes. Remove from pan and allow to cool completely before frosting or decorating.

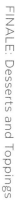

**THE GREATEST
SHOWMAN**
also *Alice in Wonderland*
or *Muppets Most Wanted*

MAKES ABOUT 5 CUPS,
enough to frost a
2-layer 9-inch cake
or 24 cupcakes

1 cup thawed frozen strawberries

1 cup (2 sticks) salted butter

6 cups confectioners' sugar

1 teaspoon vanilla extract

Heavy cream (optional)

Sideshow Strawberry Frosting

Not to compete with the main attraction, this thick and creamy strawberry frosting is the icing on the cake of any carnival or tea party. Tinted pink from the puree of frozen fruit, the frosting whips up decadent, almost like strawberry ice cream.

Piped on top of tiny cupcakes or on the layers of a cake, this strawberry frosting helps shine the light on any viewing of The Greatest Showman, Alice in Wonderland, *or* Muppets Most Wanted.

In a food processor, puree the strawberries and set aside. Note: You won't be using all the puree in this recipe. Keep this in mind before adding the strawberries to the frosting.

In the bowl of a stand mixer fitted with the paddle attachment, beat the butter on medium speed until light and creamy. Decrease the speed to low and gradually add in the confectioners' sugar, scraping down the sides, then stirring the frosting by hand. Fold in 3 tablespoons of pureed strawberries and the vanilla and increase the speed to medium-high. Beat until light and fluffy, about 3–4 minutes. If the frosting is too thick, add in more strawberry puree or a small amount of heavy cream.

THE GREATEST
SHOWMAN
also *The Sound of Music*
or *Beauty and the Beast*

MAKES 1½–2 CUPS
OF EACH SAUCE

Caramel Sauce
½ cup (1 stick) unsalted butter

½ cup brown sugar

½ cup granulated sugar

½ cup heavy cream

1 teaspoon vanilla extract

1 teaspoon baking soda

1 teaspoon kosher salt

Hot Fudge Sauce
½ cup (1 stick) unsalted butter

1 cup heavy cream

¾ cup cocoa powder

1 cup granulated sugar

½ cup chocolate chips

½ teaspoon kosher salt

2 teaspoons vanilla extract

Barnum's Salted Caramel Sauce

No candy thermometer to caramelize sugar? Not a problem. This caramel sauce requires nothing but a pot, spoon, and very few ingredients. Using cream helps this sauce mix up quick and creamy. The additional sprinkling of salt highlights the buttery and sweet flavor.

Great over Pickpocket Cardamom Bread Pudding (see recipe on page 19) or ice cream, this caramel sauce is a decadent finish to any dessert.

In a saucepan, melt the butter over medium heat. Add in the brown sugar, granulated sugar, cream, and baking soda. Stir frequently until boiling. Once bubbly, continue to stir for 1 minute, then take off the heat. Next, mix in the vanilla and salt. Serve warm or at room temperature. The sauce will thicken a bit as it cools.

Showstopper Hot Fudge Sauce

Why settle for poor and artificial-tasting store-bought chocolate sauce when the ingredients for homemade hot fudge may already be in your pantry? Made by boiling cream, butter, chocolate, and cocoa, this showstopping condiment is a star performer.

Smooth, fudgy, and gooey, the chocolatey topping can be served warm over ice cream or desserts. Leftovers are great stored in the refrigerator for another time. Warning: Even chilled, this hot fudge is tempting. It cools up thick and solid, the perfect consistency for a late-night spoonful here and there . . . just ask the sneaky kids.

In a medium saucepan over medium heat, melt the butter. Whisk in the cream. Add the cocoa powder, sugar, chocolate chips, and salt. Continue to whisk and cook until mixture is bubbly, about 3–5 minutes. Remove from heat and stir in the vanilla.

Serve warm or at room temperature. As the sauce cools, it will thicken. Refrigerate any remaining sauce and reheat again to serve.

MAKES 3 CUPS

1½ cups cold heavy cream

1 teaspoon vanilla extract

3 tablespoons confectioners' sugar

Big Top Whipped Cream

Light as air, and with the greatest of ease, this whipped cream floats through the clouds like a flying trapeze. As the final touch to pies, ice cream shakes, or cakes, this homemade topping has a place in many desserts. For a fast batch, freeze the mixing bowl. A cold bowl helps chill the cream so it whips up quick and easy.

In the bowl of a stand mixer fitted with the whisk attachment, whip the cream on medium-high speed until soft peaks form, about 3 minutes. Add in the vanilla and confectioners' sugar and continue to whisk for another 2–3 minutes. The peaks will be stiffer. Use immediately or cover and store in the refrigerator.

Index

Anatevka Potato Latkes, 47
avocados
    San Ángel Guacamole, 68
    Under the Californian Sea Sushi Rolls, 98

Babe's Brown Butter Rice Cereal Treats, The, 127
bacon
    Caramel Bacon Hello Dollies, 135
    Garden Envy Cauliflower Soup with
       Hazelnuts, 48
    Henry Higgins's Proper Full English, 15
    We Finish Each Other's Turkey, Ham, and
       Bacon Club Sandwiches, 122
Baked Alaska Ice Cream Cake, 128
Baked Banana Blueberry Oatmeal, 35
Baked Beans, You'll Be Back British, 63
Baklava Bars, Mount Olympus Orange Honey,
   151
Banana Blueberry Oatmeal, Baked, 35
Banana Bread, No Worries, 31
bananas
    Baked Banana Blueberry Oatmeal, 35
    Dandy Dan's Banoffee Pie, 139
    No Worries Banana Bread, 31
    Warm Hugs Frozen Cocoa, 91
Banoffee Pie, Dandy Dan's, 139
Barnum's Salted Caramel Sauce, 159
Baroque French Toast Sticks, 11
beans
    Henry Higgins's Proper Full English, 15
    You'll Be Back British Baked Beans, 63
beef
    Boat Snack Loco Moco, 109
    Emerald Isle Shepherd's Pie, 97
    Hermes's Greek Meatballs, 110

beverages, 82–93
    Christmas Town Hot Cocoa Mix, 87
    Club Car Malted Milkshakes, 92
    Pink Lady Lemonade, 83
    SkyDome Strawberry Milk, 84
    T-Birds' Rockin' Chocolate Cherry Coke Float,
       88
    Warm Hugs Frozen Cocoa, 91
Big Top Whipped Cream, 160
blueberries
    Baked Banana Blueberry Oatmeal, 35
    Violet's Blueberry Hand Pies, 131
Blueberry Hand Pies, Violet's, 131
Blueberry Oatmeal, Baked Banana, 35
Boat Snack Loco Moco, 109
Bob Cratchit's Smooth Mashed Potatoes, 39
Bread Pudding, Pickpocket Cardamom, 19
bread(s)
    Frog Prince Toad in the Hole, 32
    Henry Higgins's Proper Full English, 15
    I Am the Pumpkin King Bread, 16
    Let's Twist Cinnamon Sugar Donut Bites, 20
    No Worries Banana Bread, 31
    One Last Time Honey Hoe Cakes, 28
    Pickpocket Cardamom Bread Pudding, 19
    Spoonful of Sugar Strawberry Drop Scones, 23
    We Finish Each Other's Turkey, Ham, and
       Bacon Club Sandwiches, 122
breakfast, 8–35
    Baked Banana Blueberry Oatmeal, 35
    Baroque French Toast Sticks, 11
    Frog Prince Toad in the Hole, 32
    Good Morning Puffy Oven Pancakes, 12
    Henry Higgins's Proper Full English, 15
    I Am the Pumpkin King Bread, 16

Lazy Morning Congee, 27
Let's Twist Cinnamon Sugar Donut Bites, 20
Maui's Coconut Syrup, 24
No Worries Banana Bread, 31
One Last Time Honey Hoe Cakes, 28
Pickpocket Cardamom Bread Pudding, 19
Spoonful of Sugar Strawberry Drop Scones, 23
British Baked Beans, You'll Be Back, 63
Brown Butter Rice Cereal Treats, The Babe's, 127
Burgers, Polar Turkey, 114
Butter Boiled Potatoes, King Brian's, 52

Caramel Bacon Hello Dollies, 135
Caramel Sauce, Barnum's Salted, 159
Cardamom Bread Pudding, Pickpocket, 19
carrots
    Emerald Isle Shepherd's Pie, 97
    Hawaiian Mac Salad, 56
Cast Iron Skillet Chocolate Chip Cookie, 140
Castle Feast Lemon Vinaigrette, 55
Cauliflower Soup with Hazelnuts, Garden Envy, 48
cheese
    Fat Sam's Grand Slam Chicken Parmesan, 106
    Going the Distance Feta Cheese Fries, 59
    Polar Turkey Burgers, 114
    Santa Cecilia Street Corn Cups, 44
    We Finish Each Other's Turkey, Ham, and
        Bacon Club Sandwiches, 122
Cherry Coke Float, T-Birds' Rockin' Chocolate, 88
chicken
    Edna's Crispy Chicken Cutlets, 105
    Fat Sam's Grand Slam Chicken Parmesan, 106
    Jade Rabbit's Honey Soy Glazed Chicken, 113
    Triton's Salade Niçoise, 60
    Von Trapp Schnitzel with Noodles, 117
Chicken, Jade Rabbit's Honey Soy Glazed, 113
Chicken Cutlets, Edna's Crispy, 105
Chicken Parmesan, Fat Sam's Grand Slam, 106
Chocolate Cake, One More Slice, 132
Chocolate Cherry Coke Float, T-Birds' Rockin,' 88
Chocolate Chip Cookie, Cast Iron Skillet, 140
chocolate chips
    Caramel Bacon Hello Dollies, 135

Cast Iron Skillet Chocolate Chip Cookie, 140
Chocolate River Torte, 136
Headmistress Homemade Chocolate Hobnobs, 148
I Am the Pumpkin King Bread, 16
No Worries Banana Bread, 31
Phil's Peppermint Pretzel Bark, 79
Chocolate Hobnobs, Headmistress Homemade, 148
Chocolate River Torte, 136
Christmas Town Hot Cocoa Mix, 87
Cinnamon Sugar Donut Bites, Let's Twist, 20
Club Car Malted Milkshakes, 92
Club Sandwiches, We Finish Each Other's
    Turkey, Ham, and Bacon, 122
coconut
    Caramel Bacon Hello Dollies, 135
    High Tide Coconut Butter Mochi, 143
Coconut Butter Mochi, High Tide, 143
coconut milk
    High Tide Coconut Butter Mochi, 143
    Maui's Coconut Syrup, 24
Coconut Syrup, Maui's, 24
Congee, Lazy Morning, 27
Cookies, Shortbread Finger, 152
Corny's Crab Cakes with Tartar Sauce, 43
crab
    Corny's Crab Cakes with Tartar Sauce, 43
    Under the Californian Sea Sushi Rolls, 98
Crab Cakes with Tartar Sauce, Corny's, 43
Creamy Dreamy Hummus, 67
Crispy Chicken Cutlets, Edna's, 105
Crushed Cookie Frosting, Gray Stuff, 144
cucumbers
    The Muses' Cucumber Yogurt Tzatziki, 76
    Triton's Salade Niçoise, 60
    Under the Californian Sea Sushi Rolls, 98
Cucumber Yogurt Tzatziki, The Muses', 76
Cupcakes, Very Vanilla Unbirthday, 152

Dandy Dan's Banoffee Pie, 139
desserts, 125–61
    The Babe's Brown Butter Rice Cereal Treats, 127
    Baked Alaska Ice Cream Cake, 128
    Barnum's Salted Caramel Sauce, 159

Big Top Whipped Cream, 160
Caramel Bacon Hello Dollies, 135
Cast Iron Skillet Chocolate Chip Cookie, 140
Chocolate River Torte, 136
Dandy Dan's Banoffee Pie, 139
Gray Stuff Crushed Cookie Frosting, 144
Headmistress Homemade Chocolate Hobnobs,
    148
High Tide Coconut Butter Mochi, 143
Mount Olympus Orange Honey Baklava Bars,
    151
One More Slice Chocolate Cake, 132
Shortbread Finger Cookies, 152
Showstopper Hot Fudge Sauce, 159
Sideshow Strawberry Frosting, 156
That Guy We Don't Talk About's Triple Milk
    Rice Pudding, 147
Very Vanilla Unbirthday Cupcakes, 152
Violet's Blueberry Hand Pies, 131
Deviled Eggs, The March Hare's, 71
Donut Bites, Let's Twist Cinnamon Sugar, 20
dressings. *See* sides, salads, and dressings

Edamame, Red Panda Angry, 72
Edna's Crispy Chicken Cutlets, 105
eggs
    Frog Prince Toad in the Hole, 32
    Henry Higgins's Proper Full English, 15
    The March Hare's Deviled Eggs, 71
    Triton's Salade Niçoise, 60
    Uncle Albert Bubble and Squeak Patties, 121
Emerald Isle Shepherd's Pie, 97
entrees, 94–123
    Boat Snack Loco Moco, 109
    Edna's Crispy Chicken Cutlets, 105
    Emerald Isle Shepherd's Pie, 97
    Fat Sam's Grand Slam Chicken Parmesan, 106
    Hermes's Greek Meatballs, 110
    Jade Rabbit's Honey Soy Glazed Chicken, 113
    Kalua Pulled Pork, 102
    Lunchtime Spam Musubi, 101
    Polar Turkey Burgers, 114
    Selkie's Secret Pan-Fried Fish, 118
    Uncle Albert Bubble and Squeak Patties, 121
    Under the Californian Sea Sushi Rolls, 98
    Von Trapp Schnitzel with Noodles, 117

We Finish Each Other's Turkey, Ham, and
    Bacon Club Sandwiches, 122

Fat Sam's Grand Slam Chicken Parmesan, 106
Feta Cheese Fries, Going the Distance, 59
Finger Cookies, Shortbread, 152
Fish, Selkie's Secret Pan-Fried, 118
fish and seafood
    Corny's Crab Cakes with Tartar Sauce, 43
    Selkie's Secret Pan-Fried Fish, 118
    Triton's Salade Niçoise, 60
    Under the Californian Sea Sushi Rolls, 98
French Toast Sticks, Baroque, 11
Fried Wonton Moons, 75
Fries, Going the Distance Feta Cheese, 59
Fries, Hakuna Yamatata Berbere, 51
Frog Prince Toad in the Hole, 32
Frozen Cocoa, Warm Hugs, 91
Full English, Henry Higgins's Proper, 15

Garden Envy Cauliflower Soup with Hazelnuts,
    48
Ginger Orange Dressing, Guardian, 40
Going the Distance Feta Cheese Fries, 59
Good Morning Puffy Oven Pancakes, 12
Gray Stuff Crushed Cookie Frosting, 144
ground beef
    Boat Snack Loco Moco, 109
    Emerald Isle Shepherd's Pie, 97
    Hermes's Greek Meatballs, 110
Guacamole, San Ángel, 68
Guardian Ginger Orange Dressing, 40

Hakuna Yamatata Berbere Fries, 51
Hand Pies, Violet's Blueberry, 131
Hawaiian Mac Salad, 56
Hazelnuts, Garden Envy Cauliflower Soup with,
    48
Headmistress Homemade Chocolate Hobnobs, 148
Hello Dollies, Caramel Bacon, 135
Henry Higgins's Proper Full English, 15
Hermes's Greek Meatballs, 110
High Tide Coconut Butter Mochi, 143
Hobnobs, Headmistress Homemade Chocolate,
    148
Hoe Cakes, One Last Time Honey, 28

Honey Hoe Cakes, One Last Time, 28
Honey Soy Glazed Chicken, Jade Rabbit's, 113
Hot Cocoa Mix, Christmas Town, 87
Hummus, Creamy Dreamy, 67

I Am the Pumpkin King Bread, 16
Ice Cream Cake, Baked Alaska, 128
ingredients, essential, 6

Jade Rabbit's Honey Soy Glazed Chicken, 113

Kalua Pulled Pork, 102
Kettle Corn, Ringmaster, 80
King Brian's Butter Boiled Potatoes, 52
kitchen tools, 7

Latkes, Anatevka Potato, 47
Lazy Morning Congee, 27
Lemonade, Pink Lady, 83
Lemon Vinaigrette, Castle Feast, 55
Let's Twist Cinnamon Sugar Donut Bites, 20
Lunchtime Spam Musubi, 101

Mac Salad, Hawaiian, 56
main courses. *See* entrees
Malted Milkshakes, Club Car, 92
March Hare's Deviled Eggs, The, 71
Mashed Potatoes, Bob Cratchit's Smooth, 39
Maui's Coconut Syrup, 24
Meatballs, Hermes's Greek, 110
Milkshakes, Club Car Malted, 92
Mochi, High Tide Coconut Butter, 143
Mount Olympus Orange Honey Baklava Bars, 151
Muses' Cucumber Yogurt Tzatziki, The, 76

Niçoise, Triton's Salade, 60
nori
    Lunchtime Spam Musubi, 101
    Under the Californian Sea Sushi Rolls, 98
No Worries Banana Bread, 31

Oatmeal, Baked Banana Blueberry, 35
One Last Time Honey Hoe Cakes, 28
One More Slice Chocolate Cake, 132
Orange, Guardian Ginger, Dressing, 40

Orange Honey Baklava Bars, Mount Olympus, 151

Pancakes, Good Morning Puffy Oven, 12
pantry items, 6
pasta
    Hawaiian Mac Salad, 56
    Von Trapp Schnitzel with Noodles, 117
Peppermint Pretzel Bark, Phil's, 79
Phil's Peppermint Pretzel Bark, 79
Pickpocket Cardamom Bread Pudding, 19
Pink Lady Lemonade, 83
Polar Turkey Burgers, 114
pork
    Emerald Isle Shepherd's Pie, 97
    Hermes's Greek Meatballs, 110
    Kalua Pulled Pork, 102
Pork, Kalua Pulled, 102
potatoes
    Anatevka Potato Latkes, 47
    Bob Cratchit's Smooth Mashed Potatoes, 39
    Emerald Isle Shepherd's Pie, 97
    Going the Distance Feta Cheese Fries, 59
    King Brian's Butter Boiled Potatoes, 52
    Triton's Salade Niçoise, 60
    Uncle Albert Bubble and Squeak Patties, 121
Potatoes, King Brian's Butter Boiled, 52
Potato Latkes, Anatevka, 47
Pretzel Bark, Phil's Peppermint, 79
Pulled Pork, Kalua, 102
Pumpkin King Bread, I Am the, 16

Red Panda Angry Edamame, 72
rice
    Boat Snack Loco Moco, 109
    Lazy Morning Congee, 27
    Lunchtime Spam Musubi, 101
    That Guy We Don't Talk About's Triple Milk
        Rice Pudding, 147
    Under the Californian Sea Sushi Rolls, 98
Rice Cereal Treats, The Babe's Brown Butter, 127
Rice Pudding, That Guy We Don't Talk About's
    Triple Milk, 147
Ringmaster Kettle Corn, 80

Salade Niçoise, Triton's, 60
salads. *See* sides, salads, and dressings
Salted Caramel Sauce, Barnum's, 159
San Ángel Guacamole, 68
Sandwiches, We Finish Each Other's Turkey,
    Ham, and Bacon Club, 122
Santa Cecilia Street Corn Cups, 44
Schnitzel with Noodles, Von Trapp, 117
Scones, Spoonful of Sugar Strawberry Drop, 23
seafood. *See* fish and seafood
Selkie's Secret Pan-Fried Fish, 118
Shepherd's Pie, Emerald Isle, 97
Shortbread Finger Cookies, 152
Showstopper Hot Fudge Sauce, 159
sides, salads, and dressings, 36–63
    Anatevka Potato Latkes, 47
    Bob Cratchit's Smooth Mashed Potatoes, 39
    Castle Feast Lemon Vinaigrette, 55
    Corny's Crab Cakes with Tartar Sauce, 43
    Garden Envy Cauliflower Soup with
        Hazelnuts, 48
    Going the Distance Feta Cheese Fries, 59
    Guardian Ginger Orange Dressing, 40
    Hakuna Yamatata Berbere Fries, 51
    Hawaiian Mac Salad, 56
    King Brian's Butter Boiled Potatoes, 52
    Santa Cecilia Street Corn Cups, 44
    Triton's Salade Niçoise, 60
    You'll Be Back British Baked Beans, 63
Sideshow Strawberry Frosting, 156
SkyDome Strawberry Milk, 84
snacks, 66–81
    Creamy Dreamy Hummus, 67
    Fried Wonton Moons, 75
    The March Hare's Deviled Eggs, 71
    The Muses' Cucumber Yogurt Tzatziki, 76
    Phil's Peppermint Pretzel Bark, 79
    Red Panda Angry Edamame, 72
    Ringmaster Kettle Corn, 80
    San Ángel Guacamole, 68
Spam Musubi, Lunchtime, 101
Spoonful of Sugar Strawberry Drop Scones, 23
staple ingredients, 6
strawberries
    Sideshow Strawberry Frosting, 156

SkyDome Strawberry Milk, 84
    Spoonful of Sugar Strawberry Drop Scones, 23
Strawberry Drop Scones, Spoonful of Sugar, 23
Strawberry Frosting, Sideshow, 156
Strawberry Milk, SkyDome, 84
Street Corn Cups, Santa Cecilia, 44
Sushi Rolls, Under the Californian Sea, 98

Tartar Sauce, Corny's Crab Cakes with, 43
T-Birds' Rockin' Chocolate Cherry Coke Float, 88
That Guy We Don't Talk About's Triple Milk Rice
    Pudding, 147
Toad in the Hole, Frog Prince, 32
tomatoes
    Fat Sam's Grand Slam Chicken Parmesan, 106
    Henry Higgins's Proper Full English, 15
    San Ángel Guacamole, 68
    Triton's Salade Niçoise, 60
Torte, Chocolate River, 136
Triple Milk Rice Pudding, That Guy We Don't
    Talk About's, 147
Triton's Salade Niçoise, 60
turkey
    Polar Turkey Burgers, 114
    We Finish Each Other's Turkey, Ham, and
        Bacon Club Sandwiches, 122
Turkey Burgers, Polar, 114
Tzatziki, The Muses' Cucumber Yogurt, 76

Unbirthday Cupcakes, Very Vanilla, 152
Uncle Albert Bubble and Squeak Patties, 121
Under the Californian Sea Sushi Rolls, 98

Vanilla Unbirthday Cupcakes, Very, 152
Very Vanilla Unbirthday Cupcakes, 152
Violet's Blueberry Hand Pies, 131
Von Trapp Schnitzel with Noodles, 117

Warm Hugs Frozen Cocoa, 91
We Finish Each Other's Turkey, Ham, and Bacon
    Club Sandwiches, 122
Whipped Cream, Big Top, 160
Wonton Moons, Fried, 75

You'll Be Back British Baked Beans, 63

Musical Index

Alice in Wonderland
    Christmas Town Hot Cocoa Mix, 87
    I Am the Pumpkin King Bread, 16
    The March Hare's Deviled Eggs, 71
    No Worries Banana Bread, 31
    One More Slice Chocolate Cake, 132
    Sideshow Strawberry Frosting, 156
    SkyDome Strawberry Milk, 84
    Spoonful of Sugar Strawberry Drop Scones, 23
    Very Vanilla Unbirthday Cupcakes, 152
    Violet's Blueberry Hand Pies, 131
Annie, 39, 128, 132

Beauty and the Beast
    Barnum's Salted Caramel Sauce, 159
    Baroque French Toast Sticks, 11
    Big Top Whipped Cream, 159
    Garden Envy Cauliflower Soup with
        Hazelnuts, 48
    Gray Stuff Crushed Cookie Frosting, 144
    Showstopper Hot Fudge Sauce, 159
    Triton's Salade Niçoise, 60
Book of Life, The, 44, 68
Bugsy Malone, 105, 106, 139, 159

Coco, 44, 68, 147

Darby O'Gill and the Little People, 35, 52, 97

Encanto, 147

Fiddler on the Roof, 47, 67
Frozen, 91, 122

Grease, 83, 88, 92, 114, 159

Greatest Showman, The
    Barnum's Salted Caramel Sauce, 159
    Big Top Whipped Cream, 159
    Pink Lady Lemonade, 83
    Ringmaster Kettle Corn, 80
    Showstopper Hot Fudge Sauce, 159
    Sideshow Strawberry Frosting, 156
    T-Birds' Rockin' Chocolate Cherry Coke Float,
        88

Hairspray, 20, 43, 105, 127
Hamilton, 28, 32, 63
Hello Dolly! 135
Hercules, 59, 67, 76, 110, 151
High School Musical, 114, 128
Hocus Pocus, 152

Into the Woods, 44

Labyrinth, 127
Lilo & Stitch
    Boat Snack Loco Moco, 109
    Hawaiian Mac Salad, 56
    High Tide Coconut Butter Mochi, 143
    Kalua Pulled Pork, 102
    Lunchtime Spam Musubi, 101
Lion King, The, 31, 51
Little Mermaid, The, 43, 60, 98, 118

Mary Poppins, 23, 63, 121, 139
Mary Poppins Returns, 15
Matilda, 63, 132, 148
Moana
    Boat Snack Loco Moco, 109

Fried Wonton Moons, 75
Hawaiian Mac Salad, 56
High Tide Coconut Butter Mochi, 143
Kalua Pulled Pork, 102
Lunchtime Spam Musubi, 101
Maui's Coconut Syrup, 24
Mulan, 27, 40, 75, 113
Muppets Most Wanted, 127, 152, 156
My Fair Lady, 15, 121, 136

Nightmare Before Christmas, The
Chocolate River Torte, 136
Christmas Town Hot Cocoa Mix, 87
I Am the Pumpkin King Bread, 16
The March Hare's Deviled Eggs, 71
Phil's Peppermint Pretzel Bark, 79
Shortbread Finger Cookies, 152

Oliver! 19, 27
Over the Moon, 113

Princess and the Frog, 28, 32

Scrooge, 27, 39
Singin' in the Rain, 11, 12, 24, 28, 32

Song of the Sea
Baked Banana Blueberry Oatmeal, 35
Bob Cratchit's Smooth Mashed Potatoes, 39
Emerald Isle Shepherd's Pie, 97
Headmistress Homemade Chocolate Hobnobs, 148
King Brian's Butter Boiled Potatoes, 52
Selkie's Secret Pan-Fried Fish, 118
Spoonful of Sugar Strawberry Drop Scones, 23
Sound of Music, The, 12, 105, 117, 159

Tangled, 48, 140
That Thing You Do, 71
Turning Red
Guardian Ginger Orange Dressing, 40
Jade Rabbit's Honey Soy Glazed Chicken, 113
Lazy Morning Congee, 27
Let's Twist Cinnamon Sugar Donut Bites, 20
Red Panda Angry Edamame, 72
SkyDome Strawberry Milk, 84

White Christmas, 79, 83, 92, 122
Willy Wonka and the Chocolate Factory, 131, 136